Nonprofit Work Is Killin' Me

T0247627

Nonprofit Work Is Killin' Me

Mitigating Chronic Stress and Vicarious Trauma in Social Service Organizations

MORGHAN VÉLEZ YOUNG

Toplight

Jefferson, North Carolina

LIBRARY OF CONGRESS CATALOGUING-IN-PUBLICATION DATA

Names: Vélez Young, Morghan, 1984– author.
Title: Nonprofit work is killin' me : mitigating chronic stress and vicarious trauma in social service organizations / Morghan Vélez Young.
Other titles: Nonprofit work is killing me
Description: Jefferson, North Carolina : Toplight, 2023 |
Includes bibliographical references and index.
Identifiers: LCCN 2022059889 | ISBN 9781476680002 (paperback : acid free paper) ∞
ISBN 9781476647531 (ebook)
Subjects: LCSH: Social service—Psychological aspects. | Social workers—Psychology. |
Stress management. | BISAC: SELF-HELP / Self-Management / Stress Management
Classification: LCC HV41 .V45 2023 | DDC 344.03—dc23/eng/20230118
LC record available at https://lccn.loc.gov/2022059889

BRITISH LIBRARY CATALOGUING DATA ARE AVAILABLE

ISBN (print) 978-1-4766-8000-2
ISBN (ebook) 978-1-4766-4753-1

Front cover image © kalavart/Shutterstock

Printed in the United States of America

Toplight is an imprint of McFarland & Company, Inc., Publishers

Box 611, Jefferson, North Carolina 28640
www.toplightbooks.com

To all nonprofit colleagues;
their wisdom and perseverance has informed
the best parts of my commitment and dreams
for transforming our shared future.

Table of Contents

Preface

Those of us working in nonprofit community-based organizations center our lives on transforming racism and classism, its symptoms and foundations. While many of our organizations don't make claim to this in the official website listed organizational mission statements, it is implied by the content of our programming, services, and strategies, confirming that we are triaging and healing -isms. Yet, our attentiveness to perceiving and transforming racism and classism outwardly through our community work must not blind us to this same work inwardly where racism and classism inside of our organizations leaves us injured among ourselves. This book furthers a conversation about what's killin' many of us through the course of our daily work lives, that of the unmitigated chronic stress and vicarious trauma identifiable within the nuances of our job descriptions and the health of our bodies. This book is written with unending love for nonprofit community-based organizations and the people who comprise them; this book was inspired by the ingenious professionals who I call friends and family.

Many friends hold claim over this book title, making clever quips of various sorts, proposing humorous word combinations over the course of our years serving together. Their intelligence and humility shine through the ways that they activate and amplify transformation across communities. I have been truly fortunate to learn from the actions and ways of my colleagues as we collectively coordinate possibilities with the masses. It is said that Raven got its color from the scorching endured when Raven was the first to try to grab and bring fire back for all. This took place long before we widely used fire on the planet and such a feat had not yet been attempted. Raven's feathers were charred while willingly extending use of its size and skills to retrieve fire. After Raven, several more each took their turns to try to do the same. I know all of them, Raven, the Owls, Snake, and Water Spider for I have seen them all in the laughter, presentations, sick days, program launches, and creative ideas brainstormed by text messages and long walks. I have seen many Ravens, Owls, Snakes, and Water Spiders enter into the fire zone of their job roles because there is something important to bring forth that can serve thousands more. However, this willingness, this humility, is manipulated by the freedom in which white supremacy culture directs the course of the internal workings of our organizations.

This book was written across three years and during life circumstances that bring many of us to our knees, including family crises, a pandemic, and the intensification of how social inequities get magnified during such situations (e.g., domestic violence, housing loses, mass incarceration, and health failures). The transformative promises that inspire our dedication to these jobs sometimes requires scorching. Without enacting our values outwardly *and* inwardly, however, the tendency towards dedication and humility for transforming our communities gets toyed with by the powerful components of white supremacy culture. The links between these cultural norms and beliefs and unmitigated chronic stress and vicarious trauma inside of our organizations is carefully explored throughout this book. Those of us, most of us, who carry white supremacy culture in our bodies, families, spirits, speech, relationships, whether we are in Black, Red, Brown, Yellow, and/or white identities, are so used to it (Menakem, 2017), so much so that the white supremacy values of efficiency, professionalism, defensiveness, fragility, sense of urgency, and so forth go unnoticed (Okun, n.d.). This is the power of any culture's norms and beliefs and I crafted this book with the awareness of how easily its pages can be co-opted in the writing and reading of it.

The thing is, none of our lives are said to matter much in a white supremacy culture; while white identities are prioritized in economics, politics, medicine, etc., in this country, there is no intrinsic value attached to their lives, only to the power that whiteness wields. And many of us have seen white sisters and brothers thrown away for their allyship with those of us navigating beneath layers of oppression. It is important to understand that; power is promoted for displays of whiteness in the white supremacy cultural beliefs and norms inside of our organizations. These tendencies produce community-based organizations with high levels of unmitigated chronic stress and vicarious trauma that is spread out among all of us, though some of our bodies suffer more while some can ignore it. The bodies of greatest concern that drive this book's conversation are those in direct service job roles walking alongside community members. These professionals are primarily in nonprofit community-based social services organizations, but also include organizations with programming that resembles social services but which is only one approach in their movement-building investments.

Preface

My family and ancestors show us another way. The Owls, Snake, and Water Spider joined Raven to bring back fire; they saw a transformational opportunity before them. Through our relationships with one another in community work, we, too, take our turns towards contributing to shared visions. We can see aspects of Raven, the Owls, Snake, and Water Spider in our actions. We are relational and, therefore, we are valuable in our community work outside of the punishing tendencies of white supremacy culture. Nonprofit community-based professionals are relational as a requirement for the transformation that we crave to be a part of; our individual and collective value blooms in obvious ways from this work like flowers from concrete. We are not simply making transactions among people and things. My role in writing this book is amalgamizing the talent and insights fed to me through our turn-taking, relationships, and shared commitments in community work. Taking a turn, here, by offering a resource in *Nonprofit Work Is Killin' Me*, I simply came up with words for book pages made possible from our relationships across this country.

The layers of our identities always involve relationships. The footprints we create each day are partially created in relationships with those we walk next to, those who crafted our shoes, those who await our arrival. My identities, too, inform how this book is presented to you. My identities elongate me, stretching the length and depth of my duty to fulfill visions created before my time, before my parents and grandparents; I wear these visions like a shawl. For me, there has only ever been this relationship with their visions. Every task, role, title, and place I have entered fulfills some part of their visions. As a daughter and granddaughter, walking in my heritages and histories translates as me wearing an awareness every day about which tasks I carry out for fulfilling their visions, whose face I see staring back at me in the mirror, and which mannerisms I display that come from strong people with very few belongings. As a sister, walking in the privacy of our shared memoirs inspires me to ask which resources I have access to in order to change the systems that pushed and pulled on us in diverse and hurtful ways. As a mother, I hold the nausea and numbness of what it is like to have children controlled by systems rather than cultivated by communities. In many spaces and seasons of life, this palpable sensory directs my attention to ask, "How can I make this situation joyful for this child in front of me?" "How can I honor this child in the midst of this difficulty?" I have asked this since I began at 22 years old working inside of youth prisons and these questions have emerged stronger as I birthed my own child. In yet another layer of my identities, as a friend to people with rich and beautiful hearts, I have received so much love through attention,

Preface

consoling, and celebration. Our reach for one another has sparked courage and permitted rest when only friendship could do that. These identities and their foundational relationships became the energy used for writing much of this book.

And yet, two more layers of my identities are often elevated and promoted in the likes of white supremacy culture. Most often, I am introduced for my Ivy League training and the works that I have authored as if these belong to me and not my family, as if they hold authority outside of their purpose. I understand this tendency, but I do prefer to be known as a daughter, granddaughter, sister, mother, and friend. As a Stanford University–trained researcher, I have learned to be quite harsh about what counts as data, who decides, and who passes as an expert. The rebellious mentors who patiently cultivated me, Ray and Guadalupe especially, were strict with me in the quality of my work and in the kindness of my heart. This pedigree, however, required wading through injurious systems. Literally, only a few years ago, nearly a decade after leaving Stanford, I put away the pearl earrings, remnants of those systems, though my mother enjoyed wearing such which complemented nicely with her hopes for anything but poverty. In the privacy of my work space, laptop, and strategy meetings, my Ivy League training and publishing history actually morphs into a tiny thread to weave in and out of the minutiae of data analysis and prepping for university classes and community trainings. My private time with data, looking through it by hand, one line at a time, cleaning, and organizing would typically be referred to as grunt work. But the intersections of my identities drive my careful attention while simultaneously honoring each person, each human, line by line through data sets before the names are removed for anonymizing and aggregating. I want to know their names; their lives matter. This is not grunt work to me but honoring lives who are letting me and the world learn something; this approach is honoring the visions of my family and ancestors. This quiet way of expressing my researcher identity allows me to scorch my feathers on the life experiences of children behind bars, families in trafficking, young adults in restorative programs, and so forth until I craft something with paper and my name on it with a time stamp for worlds where applied projects, university teaching, and writing live.

Finally, as a nonprofit professional with 20 years of social services and movement-building experiences, I carry the sarcasm, silent stares, and other traits rubbed off from peers and mentors. No matter the context, this layer of my identities always fuels me to ask, "Who does that thing really serve?" "How would that actually be implemented in the real world?" "Is this only transactional?" While I would not trade many of my social services job experiences because of how smart they made me from serving and knowing amazing community members, the measurable and unmeasurable suffering of chronic stress and vicarious trauma is part of this layer. As a literacy mentor with preschoolers, workshop facilitator in youth prisons, teen parenting trainer, case manager, foster care services coordinator, and more, I emerged among an orchard of many brilliant people with collective dedication.

While my name is on this book because I typed on the keyboard with the graces of the kind and patient Toplight publishing team, often with my son nearby, *Nonprofit Work Is Killin' Me* doesn't belong to me any more than the layers of my identities belong to me, all of which have been braided together through the voices, hearts, minds, and hands of many beautiful people. Numerous struggles in nonprofit community-based organizations stem from ignoring unmitigated chronic stress and vicarious trauma and the white supremacy cultural norms that underpin them. When our organizational mission statements can't honestly depict the purpose of our organizations to transform -isms, we shouldn't be surprised when -isms are recycled and maintained internally. Worry about external challenges to speaking openly about the purpose of our organizations is practical; funding access and political support are tremendously important to dance with for the longevity of our organizations. For many, we cannot rock the boat with any funder; if they don't like the words "decolonize," "racism," "homophobia," "Islamophobia," and so forth, then the words are removed. And yet, the swiftness with which organizations remove these words is typically the swiftness of turning their backs on their own team and leaving chronic stress and vicarious trauma to continue uninterrupted. Internal challenges to speaking truth about the presence of racism and classism inside of our organizations is so viscerally uncomfortable for many even though our organizations are full of smart and intentional people (DiAngelo, 2021; Villanueva, 2021).

This book's unique offering on the topic of workplace racism and classism is about its fueling of unmitigated chronic stress and vicarious trauma in nonprofit community-based organizations, with special attention to social services organizations, all of which are designed to curb -isms. Racism and classism unleash social issues that look like housing insecurity, food deserts, domestic violence, and more. To mitigate chronic stress and vicarious trauma is to transform the impact of societal racism and classism from running freely inside of our organizations that create symbolic versions of housing insecurity, food deserts, etc., among

Preface

professional teams. Hence, many of us rely on rooting ourselves in authentic relationships, listening, and praying with self-accountability in order to move with grace in this time. This book, also, was crafted with prayer (and other tools you'll read about in later chapters).

Exploring the science of unmitigated chronic stress and vicarious trauma helps us to understand the ways that our bodies are impacted by the jobs that we take on. The social science helps us to recognize what fuels this. My dedication to, and love for, nonprofit community-based professionals is grounded in the many smart and kind ones that I've known my whole life, including those who very early provided food boxes and winter coats for my small frame. The science-backed critiques of racism and sexism in our organizations discussed in this book adds to our lives and the transformations we are involved in.

A tremendous thank you goes to my brothers, father, and sister for your embrace across the three years of writing this book, during major crises. A big hug of gratitude goes to my compassionate and loving friends Aurora and Georgia; I love you. Thank you to my son, Sebastián, for the ways that your spirit has gifted me so much learning and love that made this book possible; my life is better because of you. Finally, my wider family and ancestors, I understand the responsibilities to give as much of myself as I have and celebrate as much as I can; everything that I have the pleasure to enjoy in this lifetime is because of the path that you laid for all of us. I love knowing that my son is your dream. And Raven, the Owls, Snake, and Water Spider, those who went first to initiate the gathering of fire at great risk, especially Water Spider who rocked it, thank you for your spirit which fueled my passion to pour into the pages of this book.

Introduction

Nonprofit Work Is Killin' Me is written for nonprofit community-based professionals on the front lines, carrying out their responsibilities for triaging and healing the challenges that stem from racism and classism. For professionals who walk alongside community members such as teen parents, families who are unhoused, persons returning from prisons, and so forth, we often experience unmitigated chronic stress and vicarious trauma through the course of fulfilling what we are hired to do. However, this book will also be useful for friends and family who would like to better understand the requirements and barriers of such transformative work. It can be seen as a cautionary preview for those who are considering a path in such challenging yet necessary settings. And this book is written for managers, executive leaders, board members, and anyone else who would like to use their influence to help edit the norms and beliefs that create unmitigated chronic stress and vicarious trauma in our organizations.

The honest conversation inside of these pages focuses on the chronic stress and vicarious trauma that is running unchecked in nonprofit community-based organizations, especially for those who are in direct service job roles. Primarily, these professionals work inside of what are referred to as nonprofit community-based social services organizations, but also include organizations with programming that is social services in its design but for which that programming is only one strategy surrounding larger movement-building plans.

This conversation is vital for understanding how the high rates of burnout and suffering in the nonprofit sector came to be and the need to transform the sector norms and beliefs that perpetuate the problem. The science and conversation are presented with earnestness for turning around the difficult experiences of, particularly, nonprofit community-based social services teams which also requires that we counter racism and classism central to the nonprofit sector culture. Ultimately, committing to and implementing solutions for mitigating chronic stress and vicarious trauma allows these teams to function coherently by

Introduction

addressing social inequities in the community and addressing the ways that these same inequities are alive inside of our organizations.

Chronic stress and vicarious trauma are weaved into the very fabric of the jobs, priorities, and settings of nonprofit community-based social services organizations. Yet, outside of consideration of the contexts of serving in emergency rooms, battlefields, classrooms, and domestic violence shelters, we do not hear about the ways that many other job roles carry the responsibility of braving chronic stress and vicarious trauma. For example, meet Lee. He works with families who are unhoused with the ultimate goal of bridging them first to temporary and then to permanent housing. Lee's job title, *screening specialist*, is nondescript, and when he shares the goal that guides his work, few in his life actually understand what it takes to fulfill his job duties in terms of the pace he moves each day as well as the impact of job tasks on his biology and quality of life.

It is important to understand the reality of Lee's responsibilities because the general public often interprets nonprofit topics in overly simplistic ways. For example, heavy attention is sometimes placed on the families' dire circumstances; of course it is very important to cultivate awareness about unhoused families. On the other end, suspicions are placed on the effectiveness of Lee and his work from donors and popular media; crude questions misplace attention about the value and accomplishments of nonprofit work with catch phrases about "overhead." Many of us have heard questions such as "Is his salary too high?" "Why are so many families still homeless if we're paying nonprofits to fix the problem?" "Will this program still exist after grant funding runs out?"

Supposed concern about overhead and the general value and accomplishments of nonprofit work in actuality reflects cultural commitments to racism and classism that permeate this country. The questions, like Lee faces, are not misplaced. Rather, they intentionally draw the public's support for diminishing the pay associated with jobs that are focused on addressing social inequities; emphasizing the assumed need for overworking the professionals who are tasked with addressing systemic oppressions like unhoused families; and suspecting that the populations directly impacted by the social inequities are in some way deserving of them.

Activating our collective drive to mitigate chronic stress

> *Getting on the Same Page*
>
> *In order to address unmitigated chronic stress and vicarious trauma in nonprofit community-based social services organizations, we must also transform the racism and classism built into the structures and practices of our precious organizations.*

8

and vicarious trauma, supported by this book, entails taking on the fundamental webbing shared among the following:

- unmitigated chronic stress and vicarious trauma;
- racism and classism in the nonprofit sector and the U.S. more widely; and
- demonstrations of mission impact and movement-building.

In order to address unmitigated chronic stress and vicarious trauma in nonprofit community-based social services organizations, we must also transform the racism and classism built into the structures and practices of our precious organizations. The shared webbing referenced here is the focus of an entire chapter so that we can all be on the same page about what is needed for curbing the blowback of unmitigated chronic stress and vicarious trauma in relation to racism, classism, missions, and movement-building.

Lee's exhaustion and exposure to chronic stress and vicarious trauma are not an individual's problem; they mirror a larger umbrella issue that is given center stage in this book because it represents the core experiences of nonprofit professionals. While the questions posed to professionals like Lee are largely treated as essential, timeless, inevitable, and reasonable questions, they actually reflect white supremacy cultural values that fixate on squeezing every ounce of production from human beings. That is, the European industrial revolution and colonization model makes it appear natural to overwork and squeeze historically oppressed populations. This culture, obviously, also invests minimally in the well-being of teams like in the case of the failure to mitigate chronic stress and vicarious trauma in nonprofit community-based social services organizations. The white supremacy cultural focus within such organizations assumes that it is natural and inevitable for organizational teams to exhibit efficiency, individualism, fear of conflict, defensiveness, and urgency no matter an organization's mission and plans (Okum, n.d.).

As a researcher and anthropologist, I know that there are few things, if any, that are essential, timeless, and inevitable, but short-term memory might have our attention easily diverted to assume these things are true; nonprofit employment models are designed to reflect white supremacy culture. It makes it unsurprising, then, that after almost two decades of working in nonprofit community-based social services roles, I have seen countless teams experience the constant hum and rhythmic beats of unmitigated chronic stress and vicarious trauma.

The overemphasis on Lee's salary and performance shows that many do not understand the magic that Lee and his colleagues make happen every day. When he finished his college degree in sociology, he went right into this job. During his college years he worked in literacy programs, serving children in under-resourced schools. He knew conceptually that working with unhoused families would prove challenging, but he was deeply passionate about the ultimate goal of generational healing that can happen with stable housing and he entered this career path with great enthusiasm.

In Lee's daily job tasks, he engages families who are referred to his program by a range of entities like schools and overflowing temporary shelters. He also engages families by doing weekly canvassing tours of encampments and parking lots that are known for staging families who are currently living in automobiles and tent-like contraptions. Whether referred to or directly recruited by Lee, Lee's top two challenges are to build rapport with families who are deathly afraid that if they share too much information then their children will be removed from them and then to face the challenge of finding open beds for the families within cities that underinvest in such housing options. To meet both of these challenges, he spends many hours thoughtfully hanging out with families to get to know them and earning their trust. For example, Lee cannot get families into shelters unless he gets their names, ages, and sexes of their children, but many parents tend to stop talking if Lee pushes too hard to get that information. Lee also spends countless hours building trusted relationships with intake staff at every shelter within the county boundaries in order to get the latest updates on open beds; this requires many conversations, tokens of appreciation like birthday gifts and surprise coffee deliveries, and meaningful exchanges like sharing program resources with another program's enrollees.

As the third largest employer in the U.S., the nonprofit sector has a large population of chronically stressed and traumatized professionals. There are some 12 million Lees out there who are making community transformation happen. Lee, like most nonprofit community-based social services professionals, is smart, creative, and driven. And like all nonprofit community-based social services professionals, and those in other types of nonprofit organizations with social services programming, the very job role that Lee fulfills consumes more than his talents and energy. The gradual pace of building rapport, human-to-human connections, is rarely measured or considered for the way it mentally, physically, and emotionally wears on a professional in this sector.

Lee's grind is physically and mentally exhausting because he is constantly on the move, strategizing solutions, skipping meals and restroom breaks, and he pours his brain and biological power into every detail. However, Lee's exhaustion is only one layer as to how his biology is taxed. Chronic stress is defined as consistent exposure to stressors with psychological consequences that "result in serious health conditions including anxiety, insomnia, muscle pain, high blood pressure and a weakened immune system" (Baum & Posluszny, 1999). Additionally, building human-to-human bonds with populations facing tremendous barriers, such as unhoused families, means that he is enmeshed in a ripe setting for vicarious trauma. When professionals experience a client's trauma through listening to their stories, reading legal case notes, and being in dangerous residential spaces (e.g., encampments), they experience what is called *vicarious trauma*. That is, vicarious trauma is defined as psychological and biological strain from exposure to a person who has, or continues to experience, trauma and/or post-traumatic stress (Hernandez-Wolfe et al., 2014).

Consider these realities of Lee's job:

- Lee sees and hears about the emotional suffering of parents who must endure the humiliation of not being able to provide for their children.
- Lee sees the quickness with which the children consume the snacks that he brings to them, recognizing their constant hunger and malnourishment.
- Lee hears about the preceding events that led to the homelessness, including domestic violence, deaths, incarcerations, layoffs, addictions, and unlucky conditions.
- Lee knows that the families are stressed about the potential of being separated, having their children taken by child protective services if they remain homeless for too long.
- Lee hears that the children are experiencing bullying at school based on peer judgment with regard to their dirty clothes and constant hunger.
- Lee drives away at the end of visiting with families emotionally struck by the contrasts that he will pick up his favorite dinner on his way home to his safe and comfortable apartment.

Notice that Lee cannot fulfill his job responsibilities unless he is exposed to the stress and trauma of the families. While arguments can be made about unnecessary job pressures that drive Lee's exhaustion such as working 50-plus hours per week with limited resources, there is no structural change that can occur to his job role to *prevent* Lee from conditions of vicarious trauma. He must walk into the world that the families live in and that movement into their spaces brings on vicarious trauma. But what of *mitigating* that exposure and its direct impact on Lee's well-being?

In many ways, this book is a love letter to Lee and those like Lee. The nonprofit job sector includes a range of diverse roles, including formalized therapeutic roles such as *therapists* and *social workers* as well as roles that supply similar social services without formal recognition such as Lee's job as a *screening specialist*. More nonprofit community-based professionals like Lee carry titles such as *case manager, workshop facilitator,* and *mentor* (Baines et al., 2002; Rzeszutek et al., 2015). The community members who are served by these professionals—children, teens, families, the elderly, the disabled, the incarcerated, and so forth—often experience post-traumatic stress from surviving strained conditions like food insecurity, violent neighborhoods, relocating as refugees from conflict zones, and surviving abuse so common in the U.S. (Sumner et al., 2015). Nonprofit community-based social services organizations are designed to resolve human suffering and the social inequities that systemically and systematically drive that suffering. The organizational teams do this by directly serving the community through triaging and/or by changing systems that create and/or enable the suffering. Ultimately, teams inside of these organizations serve stressed and traumatized community members through the course of asking professionals themselves to endure chronic stress and vicarious trauma. Hence the name of this book, *Nonprofit Work Is Killin' Me.*

> ### Many Ironies
> *These organizations serve stressed and traumatized community members by asking professionals themselves to suffer chronic stress and vicarious trauma.*

Lee and his colleagues across the U.S. are driven to resolve the stress and trauma experienced by the community members. They see a way forward and many of them understand the theories and methods of social transformation at their organization's level and movement-building through strengthening their collaborations across entities so collective coordination lines up. Many of these professionals, including you, know deep in your bones that solutions exist for each community member though, frequently, systems and practices create barriers to enacting these solutions. Your drive keeps you in contexts where there is a biological toll to be paid and chronic stress and vicarious trauma engulfs your body.

Studies on the impact of chronic stress and vicarious trauma from the therapeutic and social work professions inside and outside of nonprofit contexts include such job roles as working in domestic violence centers and serving survivors of sexual assault and sex trafficking (Ludick & Figley, 2017; Lipsky, 2018). The toll paid by such therapeutic and social work professionals includes long-term mental health issues, deteriorating personal relationships, and an increasingly hopeless worldview (Aparicio et al., 2013). Further, advocacy nonprofit professionals have received some attention from researchers on the experiences of job-related chronic stress and vicarious trauma (Gorski, 2015; Lipsky, 2019). Similar to non-therapeutic nonprofit professionals like Lee, advocacy professionals are exposed to dynamics that involve chronic stress and vicarious trauma such as frequent exposure to traumatic visuals and written content as well as to adversarial opponents (Gorski & Erakat, 2019). Importantly for the message in this book, non-licensed nonprofit community-based professionals get little attention in the public and academic realms for the ways that they are exposed to and experience chronic stress and vicarious trauma. Professionals who are not formally designated with therapeutic or emergency job titles still carry out social services job roles with exposure to stress and trauma.

Further, few studies carefully examine the experience of nonprofit professionals working in social services organizations (Baines et al., 2002). Social services are, in fact, job tasks that reflect therapy and social work–related responsibilities like Lee's case management efforts that support the transitions of families into safe housing options. A 2018 study that I conducted on nonprofit community-based social services organizations, chronic stress, and vicarious trauma borrowed insights from research in adjacent fields such as social work and healthcare where these job-based factors have already been studied at great length. Asking questions about the existence of chronic stress and vicarious trauma in nonprofit community-based social services job roles for non-social workers, non-therapists, and non-medical personnel is an important addition to the research. The study's findings inform Chapter 2 and fuel the three chapters focused on individual, organizational, and sector level tools. Chapter 2 is framed around these two questions:

- Is it possible to distinguish characteristics of chronic stress and vicarious trauma among nonprofit community-based social services professionals and correlate them to job roles?
- Which solutions to chronic stress and vicarious trauma already exist that can be used by nonprofit community-based social services organizations to mitigate chronic stress and vicarious trauma?

Introduction

While readers should check out more about this 2018 study, mentioning it at the outset of the book is important because research from adjacent sectors only allows a general understanding about the ways that nonprofit community-based jobs are tied to the psychological and biological suffering among professionals like Lee. This understanding focuses the conversation in this book without essentializing individual professionals as solely responsible for their own well-being. That is, so much popular rhetoric about well-being in the contemporary American context is framed around white bodies and commercially informed *self-care*. Self-care social media posts are frequently parroted without possible application to contexts like those of nonprofit professionals who engage in traumatizing job duties in order to contribute to social transformation. Sandwiched between their drive for solutions to social inequities and their friends' posts about soothing bubble baths to relieve the stresses of the day, nonprofit community-based social services professionals keep their heads down with no easy answers for surviving their careers (Kisner, 2017; Mitchell, 2018).

Self-help and *self-care* are predominant themes in health and well-being publications geared for professionals, including the promotion of *self-care* plans (Skovholt & Trotter-Mathison, 2011) that include encouraging more sleep, better nutrition, deep breathing, and exercise (Kanter & Sherman, 2017; Lipskey, 2018). The spectrum of formal studies and professional tips around *self-care* like these, however, often misrepresent the distinct characteristics involved in the coercive contexts that drive unmitigated chronic stress and vicarious trauma. This rhetoric shows that effective solutions exist for responding to the biological effects of chronic stress and vicarious trauma, but does not synchronize well with the job requirements imposed on nonprofit community-based social services teams. Ain't no deep breathing going to resolve the foundational white supremacy culture that ensures unmitigated chronic stress and vicarious trauma are ignored.

Many books and resources for professionals to use for releasing some of the work-based pressure tend to encourage solutions that are research backed only for some of the ways that professionals suffer. This science is important and brings legitimacy to the experiences of the professionals with chronic stress and

> ### What This Book Is Not About
> *Suggesting exercise, baths, and nutrition—as many available wellness resources for professionals do—is a misrepresentation of the communal stress and trauma that is part of nonprofit community-based social services job roles.*

14

direct or vicarious trauma. For too many decades, people, especially women, were framed as faking the very real high blood pressure, sleep challenges, never ending fatigue, body pain, and other aspects of experiencing chronic stress and vicarious trauma. That is why a chapter in this book focuses just on the scientific findings around chronic stress and vicarious trauma.

The unfolding of chronic stress and vicarious trauma is fundamentally about the accumulation of tension to the point of biological overwhelm. Suggesting exercise, baths, and nutrition—as many available wellness resources for professionals do—is a misrepresentation of the communal stress and trauma that is part of nonprofit community-based social services job roles. For example, among mental health disciplines, the terms *emotional detachment* and *emotional regulation* refer to training for professionals where they are to simultaneously serve clients, protect themselves, and apply disciplinary standards (i.e., for clients to get what they paid for with a high degree of fidelity and safety). It is argued that when professionals can regulate their emotions in the face of chronic stress and vicarious trauma scenarios, then they are protected from the biological fallout. But is this actually possible among the nonprofit community-based social services teams? The many professionals who readers meet in the pages of this book have no choice in the matter. Emotional regulation does not increase Lee's safety when he is canvassing in dangerous areas of the city. His job description says to canvas and so he does.

You may be familiar with the term *compassion fatigue*. It is understood as the physical and psychological exhaustion experienced by people, most typically assumed to be professionals, associated with serving clients where the professional can no longer empathize or build rapport with clients because of the exhaustion (Hunsaker et al., 2015). Compassion fatigue is a potential consequence of job tasks that involve chronic stress. For example, a housing coordinator might experience compassion fatigue after years of working with numerous teens who were sexually assaulted by family members and had to find emergency housing. The in-your-face daily challenges that amount to chronic stress and vicarious trauma is what the research shows is linked to compassion fatigue; fulfilling the job tasks are linked to compassion fatigue.

Further, a workshop facilitator might experience compassion fatigue along with vicarious trauma. For instance, with every workshop series that includes curriculum and activities with participants working through how to apply *community justice* values to their experiences as violent crime survivors, such a workshop facilitator has the role to listen and learn

Introduction

along with the survivors. Professionals who experience vicarious trauma, like in this instance, may reach compassion fatigue at some point in their careers even if that compassion fatigue is resolved. However, the opposite does not necessarily happen; a professional who experiences compassion fatigue may or may not experience vicarious trauma. The research suggests that when we want to explore these various terms and dynamics, most often when there is a directional link, it is vicarious trauma → compassion fatigue and/or chronic stress → compassion fatigue. These are the definitional distinctions to help clarify and that will be discussed further in Chapter 2. For example, when I worked in youth prisons in social services programming, I was gradually on my way to compassion fatigue with no knowledge of what awaited me. After six years, I could not work in the setting anymore. I stopped being able to care about the work, the colleagues, and the precious young people. A series of health issues made it hard to make it through the day. I got to this point via vicarious trauma. Now I understand that constant exposure to a locked facility with weapons, direct and indirect violence on the young people's bodies, and a losing battle to get the youth meaningful services brought on palpable chronic stress and vicarious trauma and led to what can be identified as compassion fatigue.

The experience of compassion fatigue is especially worrisome in that research shows a link between compassion fatigue and the quality and effectiveness of job duties. No longer empathizing with community members or clients creates obvious barriers to serving them. Nonprofit community-based social services organizations are bursting with talent and innovation, yet even the greatest talent is not immune to the biological impact of chronic stress and vicarious trauma.

To round out an understanding of the differences and linkages among chronic stress, vicarious trauma, and compassion fatigue, the term *burnout* should be specifically used as it is intended. *Burnout* is the last stop on the train; it equates to a great amount of unhappiness with one's job and is shown by emotional exhaustion, depersonalization of clients, loss of interest in job duties, and a desire to stop going to work (Lampert & Glaser, 2018; Seti, 2008). When team members cannot show up to work anymore, that is the culmination of long-standing factors like unmitigated chronic stress and vicarious trauma.

Lee's college friend who works in the same region, Alice, facilitates child abuse prevention workshops with parents who are flagged by child protective services for compulsory preventative support. Alice is not a family therapist, rather, her title is *workshop facilitator*. She completed her undergraduate degree in recreational studies and in the future plans to complete a master's degree in nonprofit management. Alice faces job circumstances similar to Lee that create chronic stress and vicarious trauma, including the following:

- Alice sees and hears about the suffering of parents who must endure the humiliation of a court order to attend parenting workshops.
- Alice sees the embarrassment on the faces and timidness in the bodies of the children who play in the next room while the workshops are underway.
- Alice hears fragments of the life stories of workshop participants, sprinkled throughout the eight weeks of twice-a-week sessions.
- Alice reads the court documentation that outlines the causes for parent referrals.
- Alice hears some of the children in the next room struggling to communicate without violence.
- Alice leaves these nightly workshops and her long days drained and knowing that there are countless more families to serve in a society with such high rates of child abuse and neglect [Cecil et al., 2017].

Lee and Alice rarely speak at any length about the chronic stress and vicarious trauma in their job tasks, in their bodies, and in their futures, but they and their nonprofit peers instinctually know the reality of what toll their jobs take. These experiences of chronic stress, vicarious trauma, compassion fatigue, and burnout, and in any combination, depend upon the specific job responsibilities, persons being served by the professionals, organizational structures (Rodrigues et al, 2017), and possibly organizational leadership (Shanafelt et al., 2015).

Lee and Alice keep their mouths shut about the internal workings of their organizations because they do not want to be accused of badmouthing any organization that carries an important mission. Yet from their daily responsibilities, it makes sense that Lee and Alice experience chronic stress in the course of fulfilling their job tasks as well as vicarious trauma in the course of building human-to-human connections with the community members who they serve. Both are at risk of burnout should their job setting stay unchanging. Recall that burnout is the last stop on the train and that, long before reaching burnout, professionals like Lee and Alice face so much suffering because their job roles require it and most organizations do nothing to mitigate it.

Introduction

In a 2011 study, 45 percent of nonprofit professionals reported planning to leave their employer within the next two years in proportion to the stress they experienced (Word et al., 2011). This same study found that 30 percent of nonprofit professionals were already experiencing burnout with another 20 percent of them at risk of burnout. In the study referenced earlier that I conducted in 2018, among nonprofit community-based social services professionals specifically, many were experiencing chronic stress, 15 percent to 52 percent of them, and 13 percent to 24 percent of them were experiencing vicarious trauma. Again, visit Chapter 2 for more discussion on these rates.

Why should we explore the rates of chronic stress and vicarious trauma in nonprofit community-based social services work? Since the 1990s, increasing attention has been placed on these factors by tracking them across therapeutic contexts and even in schools, but not among the Lees and Alices in the nonprofit sector. Therapists and counselors (Graham, 2012), social workers (Aparicio et al., 2013; Branson, 2019), hospice caretakers (Hotchkiss, 2018), and even teachers (Grise-Owens et al., 2017; Skovholt & Trotter-Mathison, 2011) are recognized for the job-based conditions that create this type of suffering. In nonprofit community-based organizations, there is little to no attention to the correlation between exposure to the traumatic life experiences of those we serve and the professionals' experiences with vicarious trauma. These other sectors have insights on who, how, and when chronic stress, vicarious trauma, compassion fatigue, and/or burnout show up among their employees in large part because of the health consequences that impede employer success benchmarks. By assessing and responding to employee experiences with chronic stress, for example, employers find that they can lower the rates of noncommunicative diseases, reduce medical costs and sick time, and improve productivity and outputs (Abegun & Stanciole, 2006; Page & Nilsson, 2017; Beemsterboer et al., 2009; Bubonya et al., 2017).

This book, and its focus on the talent of nonprofit community-based professionals who widely experience chronic stress and vicarious trauma, does not promote employer success benchmarks and a focus on white supremacy cultural values like productivity and outputs. Yet, much of the available research that exists on these experiences focuses on the Eurocentric industrial revolution and colonizing paradigm of production. For example, unchecked chronic stress, vicarious trauma, compassion fatigue, and/or burnout among employees across diverse occupations is linked to a myriad of problems for the employer. Employee stress levels are directly linked to absenteeism and temporary use of disability leave (Lazaridis et al., 2017; Marzec et al., 2015). For those working in chronically unsafe scenarios, such as police officers, many studies have shown the distinctively high rates of divorce, suicide and thoughts of suicide, anxiety, and depression (Sollie et al., 2017); in the area of research on those in unsafe scenarios, the focus is, thank goodness, equally about the outputs *and* the human cost.

When chronic stress and vicarious trauma are studied in, or tangential to, the nonprofit sector, light is shown on the fact that this context can reduce the quality of social services provided to community members or clients (Graham, 2012). We see the production paradigm applied here, too. When financial return and/or loss becomes part of the conversation, nonprofit leadership and philanthropic entities are all about it (Morrissette, 2016; Timm, 2016). The hit taken to the quality control inspires some sort of action for many nonprofit organizations, though often only when there is public awareness of such issues. And quality control becomes a really big deal to executive leaders and board members when it is publicly indicated through various, and sometimes embarrassing, channels.

The nonprofit sector culture and values incubate racism and classism within the organizations, yet the official organizational mission and values create a distraction by framing organizations as primarily a force for good. The data on chronic stress and vicarious trauma as well as the widespread refusal to mitigate the negative impact of such shows that organizations are not primarily about "doing good." And the fixation on doing good was birthed through racist and classist notions anyhow; more on that later. Little consideration is given to the well-being of the teams and the contrast is that often organizational values focus on resolving social inequities; commonly, nonprofit community-based organizations champion these values, but they are not inwardly turned to benefit their own teams. The conversation in this book wants to amplify our shared commitment to social transformation through the nonprofit sector in order to light a fire of change that shines on the mutuality of well-being for the people we serve and ourselves who are committed to the transformation.

Let's Agree to Agree

Prevention of chronic stress and vicarious trauma in nonprofit community-based organizations is probably impossible. As described earlier, organizations with social services programming focus on resolving human suffering through directly partnering with community members

Introduction

who are facing oppressions of various kinds. The Lees and Alices serve stressed and traumatized populations and then suffer stress and vicarious trauma akin to those who they serve. The Lees and Alices walk into the world where the community members live and their movement into these strained spaces brings on chronic stress and vicarious trauma. We must also not underestimate the pulsing chronic stress and trauma that is part of other dimensions of our lives beyond our careers such as our very personal challenges with domestic violence, layoffs, and family members who transition, but that is beyond the scope of this book.

Let us agree that chronic stress and vicarious trauma stemming from serving people and transforming social issues that we care a lot about is the consequence and requirement for being in nonprofit community-based social services organizations, especially those of us with direct service jobs. What we can do is *mitigate* the negative impact of job-based chronic stress and vicarious trauma. The cultural norm to grind until we are depleted, brought to a crawl, does not mean that these job experiences must inevitably be this way. Mitigating job-based chronic stress and vicarious trauma means decreasing some types of exposure and adding organizational and sector level strategies to heal the negative impact on our biology.

Let's also agree that compassion fatigue and burnout are preventable and/or reduceable (Duarte & Pinto-Gouveia, 2017; Demerouti, 2015; Kim & Sekol, 2014). Many studies across other sectors show that this type of prevention is possible, including for professionals working in emergency rooms, shelters, and schools. Further, organizational studies from the for-profit business sector show that non-client related stressors can be reduced, improving the work climate and experience of professionals through the implementation of best practices in terms of workloads, personnel support, and non-monetary compensations.

There are two major roadblocks to mitigating the negative impact of chronic stress and vicarious trauma in nonprofit community-based organizations. These are also roadblocks to adding meaningful strategies for resolving deeply set norms in the nonprofit sector. We have to agree that, as a sector, we want to air and eradicate these roadblocks. The first roadblock is the romanticizing of suffering in nonprofit jobs. The second roadblock complements this romanticizing by

> *We Can* Mitigate
>
> *Mitigating job-based chronic stress and vicarious trauma means decreasing some types of exposure and adding organizational and sector level strategies to heal the negative impact on our biology.*

20

essentializing *financial strain* and *limited time* as reasonable arguments against implementing tools for mitigating the negative impact of chronic stress and vicarious trauma in our organizations.

Films with famous actors serve as useful examples of how much the romanticized suffering and supposed limited monies and time permeate the expectations for nonprofit community-based organizations. The celebration of suffering often shows up in representations such as responding heroically to emergency needs, working long and worried hours, and all at the cost of their personal well-being. Movies like *Short Term 12* (CBS News Productions, 2013), starring Academy Award–winner Brie Larson, shows the psychological and biological toll on professionals working in these organizations. Larson and other actors in these roles illustrate the grueling work involved in walking in the shoes of the community members who they serve and the ways that the human-to-human connection required to fulfill their jobs negatively impacts them. And even when nonprofits get marginal attention in major films, like *Spotlight* (McCarthy et al., 2015), we also receive the message that nonprofit organizations are small, lean, and have exhausted operations facing losing battles to make the mission impact that they intend. The losing battle theme reinforces that there's no time and space for mitigating chronic stress and vicarious trauma. The romanticizing and supposed limits to monies and time distract us from a willingness to alter the white supremacy culture norms and beliefs underlining it all.

Documentaries bring viewers even closer to the existence of stress and trauma experienced by oppressed populations and the nonprofit community-based professionals dedicated to resolving social inequities. For example, the award-winning investigative documentary work of PBS' *Frontline* takes on topic areas that many of these professionals call their day jobs. The more recent *Trafficked in America* (Infobased, 2019) shows the difficulty in identifying and serving children and adults from countries trafficked into the U.S. for slave labor. The difficulty and victims are the focus of the documentary. In fact, there is a nonprofit community-based social services organizational team working on human trafficking issues just a 15-minute drive from where I am writing this book. You will learn more about this organization, and their approaches to mitigating the negative impact of chronic stress and vicarious trauma, when you get to Chapter 3.

Further, pay and operating budgets for many nonprofit community-based organizations reflect our society's level of value placed on the populations served and the professionals doing the serving. The widely popular, international short lecture series called TED Talks and TEDx have several lectures by Western specialists who speak specifically to the issue of the dynamics around romanticizing suffering and supposed limited funds and time in the nonprofit sector. For example, Nat Ware's (2013) talk titled *Free Charities from the Idea of Charity* points to the public perception and aligning pressure that nonprofit organizations should operate with a small budget and specifically with low pay for the staff teams. Further, Juanita Wheeler's (2015) Australian TEDx speech on *Busting the Charity Overhead Myth* speaks to the paradigm used by the news media and governments which places pressure on nonprofit organizations by restricting funding to them and their important work. Ultimately, both roadblocks are rooted in white supremacy values. A detailed history of the interconnectedness of racism and classism in the nonprofit sector's widespread dismissal of mitigating chronic stress and vicarious trauma is discussed in Chapter 3.

A Shared Blunt Hit

What counts as demonstrations of mission impact and movement-building must also be presented side by side with the sufferings of teams. When 52 percent and 24 percent of our nonprofit community-based social services teams are suffering with chronic stress and vicarious trauma, let's report that immediately next to the evidence of mission accomplished. There is evidence that even while experiencing terrible suffering, teams can deliver measurable social impact, and I know many of them. However, this is shown to be widely risky, cruel, and slows our transformation of the forces that create the social inequities that are central to our organizations.

We must agree to agree that there is equal relevance for services to triage real social issues (i.e., hunger, safety, and health) and for mitigating how nonprofit community-based social services professionals experience chronic stress and vicarious trauma from their jobs. This book is written for Lee, Alice, and all who are making social transformation possible through their commitments to partnering with community members to navigate historical social trauma for which we are all the heirs. You are partnering with community members to unearth and co-create solutions. For this reason, the chapters in this book are a conversation with you, an exploration of the story of suffering in nonprofit community-based organizations as well as the solutions that exist.

In Chapter 1, readers explore the nonprofit sector, surveying major terms, organizational specialties, job types, and job settings. The sector is huge and not everyone knows everyone else. This chapter helps us to focus our attention on community-based organizations with social services programming and attempts to simplify a taxonomy for the range of specializations that community-based organization lead. Chapter 1 is also educative for the new college graduates and the curious spouse who is wondering what their partner is doing in dedicating their life to social transformation. This information prepares readers for exploring the crux of the problem in future chapters.

Focusing attention on how chronic stress and vicarious trauma unfold in job roles, Chapter 2 explains the reality of nonprofit community-based social services job tasks and demands. Even seasoned professionals will read this chapter and gain an understanding of the nuances of their circumstances; reflect on their own stories; and access a little reprieve from the frequent loneliness that comes with not speaking of our shared experiences with health challenges. Those outside of the sector, as well as those in nonprofit leadership roles who have never worked in direct service jobs, will get from this chapter sobering stories that illustrate the importance of mitigating the negative impact of chronic stress and vicarious trauma.

Next, Chapter 3 further contextualizes the nonprofit sector. Nonprofit professionals will see their circumstances depicted and gain insights on the who, what, and how of sector culture issues. That's right: The nonprofit sector has a culture with thriving beliefs and norms. While there is no one Darth Vader to point the blame at for unmitigated chronic stress and vicarious trauma, there are cultural beliefs and norms that need light shown on them so that we can choose otherwise. Readers will think to themselves, *Ah ha, that's how these problems continue!* Ultimately, this chapter brings insights about the ways that the nonprofit sector fulfills white supremacy cultural beliefs and norms, making them appear normal and inevitable.

Chapters 4, 5, and 6 take readers into practical solutions that exist for them at the individual, organizational, and sector levels. Chapter 4 guides readers through curated tools for addressing the negative impact of chronic stress and vicarious trauma on the body. These are a collection of indigenous and/or science-backed tools that will interest many. Chapter 5 is geared towards organizational leaders, introducing tools for nonprofit community-based teams to address the barriers to mitigating chronic stress and vicarious trauma inside of their organizations. Chapter 6 provides sector level tools that all readers can implement. Spreading the data and amplifying calls to resolve unmitigated chronic stress and vicarious trauma is everyone's responsibility. For all three of these chapters focused on tools, there are supports provided to readers for priming one's self and one's team for meaningful tool adoption and implementation.

Chapter 1

Nonprofit Landscape

Nonprofits are the third largest employer in the U.S. comprised of 12 million professionals (Newhouse, 2018). Nonprofits include anything from the NFL to hospitals to community food pantries. However, the nonprofit professionals who are the focus of this book are those in community-based organizations in the U.S., not in other entities that carry nonprofit tax exemptions such as sports leagues, hospitals, funding agencies, and professional associations. For clarity, some in the nonprofit sector even coined the term Community Benefit Organization (CBO) to refer specifically to organizations with missions to respond to inequities in the community through social services and/or systems change strategies, basing their very purpose on "community benefit" (Gottlieb, 2009).

Laying out the job contexts for which nonprofit community-based social services professionals in community-based organizations live out their passions is foundational for understanding the normalizing of unmitigated chronic stress and vicarious trauma. While this normalizing is deconstructed elsewhere in this book, laying out the job contexts helps readers to specifically understand nonprofit community-based social services jobs.

> _Questions That Readers Will Get Answered in This Chapter_
>
> 1. _What are nonprofit community-based social services jobs?_
> 2. _How are social services delivered?_
> 3. _What are the service and program niches that exist within the nonprofit sector in addition to social services?_
> 4. _What does chronic stress and vicarious trauma have to do with different service and program niches?_

Community-based nonprofit organizations can be understood as a tapestry of various thread types, colors, and weave techniques. There are numerous things that nonprofits make their mission, including animal services, literacy, environmental protection, natural disaster relief, healthcare services, temporary housing, food access, justice system reform, education system improvements, and so on. Nonprofits with these various missions operate in various physical settings, including their own office buildings, co-working spaces, borrowed workspaces in government buildings, and even from home, parking lots, and school cafeterias when they're not being used by children. The staff teams work regular hours and odd hours, from closed offices, cubicles, open rooms with tables, cars, farm labor fields, buses, and trains.

Spouses, friends, and families gain a lot from reading this chapter, getting a peek into the lives of these badass professionals. Spouses, friends, and families of those who work in these nonprofit organizations often wonder what the heck their loved ones are doing in this sector. They see the long hours coupled with low pay and chronic sense of urgency. However, this book is actually written for Lee and Alice who you met in the introduction of this book, all of those professionals who are in nonprofit careers in order to resolve social inequities. Do Lee and Alice know how typical their experiences are? On some level, yes. However, there are many in nonprofit community-based organizations in comfortable jobs that are unclear about the daily grind of Lee, Alice,

---

Vicarious Trauma

Vicarious trauma is defined as psychological and biological strain from exposure to a person who has or continues to experience trauma and/or post-traumatic stress (Hernandez-Wolfe et al., 2014).

---

and countless more colleagues across the country in nonprofit community-based social services jobs. The comfortable jobs are not the jobs central to this book; comfortable is defined as 40 hours per week, mid-point salaries or higher with benefits, low to moderate stress, and no vicarious trauma. It would be hard to find such a comfortable job among those professionals whose careers are dedicated to hands-on social change.

Much of the work that is killin' nonprofit social service professionals is the close proximity and long-term work with populations who are navigating significant barriers and experiencing stress and trauma. In order to set the stage for understanding their work as well as their job-based suffering, this chapter is an exploration of service and program niches, job roles, and

---

What Are "Direct Service" Jobs?

Professionals in nonprofit community-based social services organizations might be in "direct service" jobs and/or hold managerial responsibilities within these organizations. Those in "direct service" partner directly with people in the community to triage and transform dire circumstances.

---

work settings. The sector is huge and not everyone knows everyone else across niches. For example, those nonprofit professionals working in environment focused organizations interact little with nonprofit community-based social services professionals; this is related to the latter group engaging in what is called "direct service" jobs where they partner directly with people in the community to triage and transform dire circumstances.

Niches among nonprofit community-based organizations—such as environmental, social service, etc.—are not perfectly segmented from one another. Some nonprofit organizations that focus on environmental justice, for instance, partner closely with members of the community to record the health costs of chemical pesticides sprayed over their homes and schools while also working with social services organizations focused on health access and case management with specialization in serving farm workers facing dangerous conditions related to toxic pesticide exposure (Alam, 2013). This close work with community members (e.g., families) and fellow nonprofits can unfold in several ways and is important to point out. Also, this book is being written at the start of the coronavirus pandemic where suffering globally and nationally intensify the work of community-based organizations. At this time, about 350,000 Americans are recorded to have died from the virus or complications associated with the virus; and globally, deaths are nearing two million (Johns Hopkins, 2020). The shutdown of schools, companies, restaurants, and even barber shops has put a major strain on food, housing, and childcare systems across the country. Like many in the nonprofit community-based social services niche, my around-the-clock work to get food deliveries from depots to food pantries and to ensure that temporary housing sites have hard fought medical face masks and non-latex gloves has made many of our career paths look less like the social services niche and more like the emergency response niche (discussed below).

The overlap across niches should be pointed out, but the niches themselves help landscape the sector. This chapter sheds light on the who, what, where, when, and how of nonprofit organizations with special attention to social services nonprofit jobs and the professionals who walk the walk in terms of the sector's commitment to solving social inequities. The information in this chapter supplies much needed information for digesting later chapters on how chronic stress and vicarious trauma take up so much room in the lives of nonprofit community-based social services professionals.

What Are Nonprofit Community-Based Social Services Jobs?

Sometimes referred to as "human services" jobs, these are careers where professionals serve specific populations with specific services or programs for which the focus is on solving social inequities. For example, case managers who serve persons who are returning to the community after completing prison sentences are needed in order to respond to the social inequity of these persons returning home to more, even lifelong punishment even though they served their time, fulfilling the punishment deemed appropriate. Yet job and housing biases against these persons, as well as set-up-to-fail parole requirements, are the inequities that the case managers are focused on resolving, one person at a time. In fact, the organizations that these professionals work in look a lot like jobs in major institutions such as K-12 education and county government–based social work. Nonprofit community-based organizations design missions that drive their work and these mission statements indicate, overtly or subtly, that the services or programs that they offer address gaps in the work or operations of these major U.S. institutions.

Examples of this gap-filling by nonprofit social services professionals includes the history of domestic violence shelters and education services as well as human trafficking intervention programs. Domestic Abuse Intervention Services (DAIS) located in Madison, Wisconsin, was invented to resolve the absence of such services. Today, institutions such as courts, hospitals, and colleges partner with nonprofits such as DAIS whose mission is to manage a shelter and implement intervention services. However, the situation continues where such services are provided through the nonprofit sector because major institutions need the talent and attention of such nonprofit teams. Another example includes an organization that serves highly overlooked children located in Central California. The organization serves children, and later their parents, who live in temporary motel housing in a high-risk human trafficking corridor. Until it was launched in 2014, the children were overlooked by their school and local government for prevention and intervention services. The organization addresses this 21st century gap.

No matter the specific focus, domestic abuse or human trafficking, the job tasks in nonprofit community-based social services careers fall into three categories: direct service, managerial, and executive leadership. In direct service roles, professionals engage people directly in any of the following ways:

1. Greeting people and assessing whether they are eligible for services is a core activity (aka "intake" or "assessment").
2. Managing people's services, or co-managing services with them, across a series of services is a major source of transforming generational impact of social inequities (aka "case work" or "case management").
3. Training or teaching in a classroom or recreational setting requires preparation and follow up (aka "workshop facilitator" or "activity coordinator").
4. Going into neighborhoods and other predetermined spaces to share about services and programs takes professionals into many dynamic spaces (aka "outreach," "recruitment," or "canvassing").
5. Supporting the evolving needs of people in a one-to-one approach is a hallmark of the nonprofit sector (aka "mentoring" or "sponsoring").

Managerial work in nonprofit community-based social services careers includes supervisor responsibilities for supporting direct service professionals. However, several more responsibilities fall here that contribute to the success of providing direct services, including the following:

1. Managing grants that fund services and programs is vital, including grant research, writing applications, and reporting deliverables to external funders (aka "grant writing" or "budget management").
2. Reviewing and summarizing data from the delivery of services and programming allows managers to understand the quality, reach, and sustained impact of those services and programs (aka "quality assurance" or "program evaluation").
3. Facilitating collaborations with other nonprofits or institutions is important for direct service tasks because with collaborative relationships, organizations can share monies as well as link up naturally aligning services across multiple organizations (aka "coalition building" or "organizing").

Executive leadership responsibilities in nonprofit community-based social services organizations include supervisor responsibilities, but like with the difference among direct services staff members and managers, there are several more tasks included in these leadership roles. The titles for this group of professionals include CEO, Executive Director, or President; Chief Operating Officer or Director of Operations; Director of Human Resources; Director of Finances; Executive Vice President or Director of

Fund Development or Resource Development; and so forth. Professionals in these careers focus heavily on the strategy for the organization in order to create a well-run home in which the direct services live. Their job titles suggest a lot about their job responsibilities, such as these tasks:

1. Externally, fundraising is vital for sustaining or growing the financial resources of the organization in order to pay staff and cover the cost of the work setting (aka "fund development").

2. Externally, maintaining public relations and communications to ensure that the public knows what the organization does brings attention to the mission and impact made in the community (aka "marketing" or "PR").

3. Internally, overseeing human resources and the culture and climate of the entire organizational team, including volunteers, is vital for staff to make magic happen every day and address the social inequities that also exist inside organizations (aka "HR").

4. Internally, facilitating and supporting the Board of Directors is a required aspect of a healthy organization and a requirement of the U.S. Internal Revenue Service (aka "BOD management").

How Are Social Services Delivered?

Meeting Alice and Lee in the Introduction of the book on-ramped readers to think about the seeming ordinariness of nonprofit community-based social services jobs. Social services are delivered directly to people, but there are various arrangements that are important to clarify. These arrangements mean everything for understanding staff exposure to the stress and trauma of populations who are navigating numerous social barriers. If we reflect on the five ways outlined above that direct services are provided to people—assessments, case management, facilitating, outreach, and mentoring—we can break down the most common scenarios that professionals experience.

Assessments with people typically occur in four spaces: in an organization's offices, in the offices or facilities of other institutions (e.g., jails or schools), in public spaces (e.g., parks), and in people's homes. Assessments are guided through the use of paper or electronic forms in order to gather basic information about people as potential program participants. The success of conducting assessments relies on rapport-building, confidentiality, and humility to ensure the dignity of all persons that the professionals engage.

Case management with people unfolds most often in prearranged spaces: in an organization's offices, in the offices or facilities of other institutions (e.g., hospitals or colleges), and in people's homes. In addition to prearranged spaces, case management often includes predetermined times (i.e., appointments), but not always. Also, direct services must mirror the clientele's contexts, including availability evenings and weekends. For example, organizations that have services and programs for working parents must design their program times, including case management, when working parents are available. Importantly, the success of case management relies on co-facilitating as a partner with people, sharing equal footing with the people being served. That is, we know today that people are the experts of their own lives.

Facilitating, training, and teaching is often focused on two things. First, the purpose of facilitation by a direct service professional is to deliver new knowledge, skills, and resources. Second, the purpose of facilitation is to cultivate an environment where the people being served identify and/or leverage their existing knowledge, skills, and resources for a specific, targeted purpose. Facilitating typically occurs in three spaces: in an organization's offices, in the offices or facilities of other institutions (e.g., jails or schools), and in other community spaces such as churches and libraries. Facilitating an activity includes a lot of preparation to ensure the best use of everyone's time, including designing and refining curriculums, prepping tools, coordinating meals when facilitating overlaps with meal times, and arranging for childcare when program participants have childcare responsibilities of their own. The success of facilitating, training, and teaching relies on the formal training of the professionals as well as rapport-building and caution to ensure dignity for all persons involved in the activity.

Outreach by nonprofit community-based social services professionals can focus on bounded areas such as neighborhoods and city limits, involve entire regions, or happen through remote strategies like online platforms and mailings. Hence, any professional with outreach in their position description may be walking the beat, driving across spaces, or strategically engaging digital spaces or email in order to reach a targeted group of people. For example, should a professional be charged with connecting for the first time with farm workers, the professional would likely partner with another organization that already specializes in partnering with farm workers. With this support, the outreach specialist would build their understanding of the population and the best ways to build rapport before the actual canvassing. Another example includes a group of professionals walking neighborhoods in the late evening where human trafficking is known to take place in order to supply information about safe sex resources. Outreach might be coupled with assessments if a service or program is designed for this purpose. However, outreach and intake assessments can occur separately. The goals and activities appear similar across these nonprofit professionals, but one team of professionals could be sharing about safe sex resources while another team of professionals has the task of reaching out to farm workers and inviting them to a series of workshops that will respond to a need. Outreach often includes leaving a piece of paper or resource in the hands of the people being engaged; a piece of paper written in the appropriate language and with the organization's contact information is most common. The success of conducting outreach relies on deep knowledge of the people being engaged, rapport-building, and safety for the professionals … as much as is possible.

Mentoring or sponsoring people typically occurs across five spaces: in organization's offices, the offices or facilities of other institutions (e.g., jails or schools), public spaces (e.g., parks), other community spaces (e.g., library), and people's homes. Mentoring and sponsoring is as formal or informal as the program is designed to be; the intentionality of the program will guide the degree of formality. For example, for children and youth, positive youth development research encourages a curriculum-style mentoring strategy with formal mentor training (McDaniel & Yarbrough, 2016). However, for adults in sobriety-focused programs, for example, informality can be more appropriate (Lawlor et al., 2014). Hence, depending on the degree of formality, there may be curricular materials, tools, and special event trips (e.g., a horse sanctuary for therapeutic purposes). The success of mentoring relies on rigorous training, lived experiences, and regular check-ins with a supervisor in order to adjust and tailor mentoring activities as needed.

What Are the Service and Program Niches Within the Sector?

Nonprofit community-based organizations can be placed into various taxonomies to display the variations within the sector. It is most helpful to think of the sector's diversity in terms of *service and program niches*. These niches are the ways that organizational missions play out in the lives of professionals and the people who they serve. Exploring the sector through service and program niches is most helpful because the basic structure of nonprofit organizations, the community-based ones, looks nearly identical in terms of lines of authority, funding sources, and use of those funds. It is important to explore the niches for what can be illuminated about social services work. Understanding the various niches helps readers to understand the ways that social services professionals come to experience chronic stress and vicarious trauma; the up close and personal exposure to the stress and trauma of the populations is integral to the job description.

The distinctions among community-based nonprofits do not fall neatly into strict categories as discussed at the outset of this chapter. Nonetheless, through this lens we can understand nonprofits as one of seven types, including

1. social services;
2. K-12 and higher education;
3. economic development;
4. advocacy and reform;
5. arts and culture;
6. environment; and
7. emergency response.

Some nonprofits provide services and programs across more than one of these niches because the combination of certain services and programs can make a bigger positive impact compared to one service and program niche alone. For example, K-12/high education and economic development programming can, together, better support stability in the lives of young adults who are historically marginalized and face barriers to living wage jobs. A powerful combination can occur when educational support such as the completion of high school diplomas is mixed with economic development support in the form of partnerships between companies that commit to hiring students who graduate from the organization's specific training program.

Nonetheless, some nonprofits deliver just one type of service and program niche such as environmental protection. With this example, it would be unusual to see some combinations of niches within a single organization, such as a nonprofit providing rigorous environmental services along with K-12 education services, but is not totally off limits. With some combinations, however, it makes sense to have staff members leading services and programs across more than two niches within their one organization. When it does happen that some staff members hold responsibilities across multiple program niches in their one organization, they typically do so because the organizational mission calls for it and salaries are paid by multiple funding sources. For instance, many in the nonprofit community-based social services world know that one full-time employee

(FTE) may have a salary funded by multiple funding channels that span the niches: 0.5 FTE from a youth mentoring grant, 0.25 FTE from an after-school program grant, and 0.25 FTE from an emergency response grant for addressing youth homelessness = 1.0 FTE.

To continue thinking about nonprofit community-based organizations as a tapestry of service and program niches, we can explore the staff experiences in their job roles. As described above, staff carry out their nonprofit community-based social services jobs while being exposed to the stress and trauma of the populations that they serve and care so much about; working closely with people who experience historical and real-time social inequities means that these people carry stress and trauma and helping to mitigate that stress and trauma is the core of the social services work. The people served and the social services professionals must connect closely—physically, mentally, and emotionally—in order to complete the expectations of the job description and to ensure the positive results for which the program is designed. Social services, as readers recall, include intake or assessments, case management, facilitation, outreach, and mentoring. The people served by such programs range across the lifespan and other demographics, and yet the inequities that the populations grapple with follow themes like homophobia, sexism, disability bias, racism, and so forth. The social services programs unfold in various contexts such as homes, community centers, and prisons. Diagram 1.1 illustrates the complexities of this service and program niche and the approaches required of staff by their very job descriptions which create constant exposure to stress and trauma, eventually becoming their own chronic stress and vicarious trauma.

Education services and programs are another niche in which to understand the nonprofit landscape and includes K-12 and higher education programs. The diversity within this niche is noticeable in the ages served by

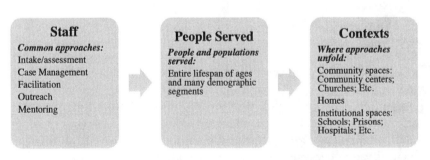

Diagram 1.1 Social services programs in nonprofit community-based organizations.

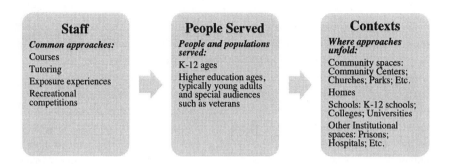

Diagram 1.2 Education services and programs in nonprofit community-based organizations.

such programs and is further complicated by the approaches used that include, but are not limited to, training courses, tutoring, exposure experiences, and recreational competitions. The ages and approaches also show up in various contexts such as school-based, literally at school sites, and community-based, which are carried out at community centers, churches, libraries, etc. Diagram 1.2 illustrates the complexities within this niche, and similar to social services programs, the approaches do bring some staff teams into the stress and trauma of the people who are served.

Economic development services and programs are yet another niche to explore in order to clarify how it is that nonprofit work is killin' professionals. This area of services and programs involves micro and meta strategies and coalition-building around a city's or region's resource development, resource allocation, and financial stability mechanisms. Partnering with formal and informal sector employees, employers, unions, city planning leadership, legislatures, and investors are central to this nonprofit niche. The people served by professionals in this niche include individuals across the lifespan and their families; most often these adults are members of historically marginalized populations such as persons with disabilities, veterans, racial/ethnic minorities, and women who are often the first to experience unemployment and/or underemployment.

The approaches used by nonprofit staff members in this niche include training courses, public convenings, and coalition building. The delivery of these approaches shows up in a few contexts, including community spaces like the offices of nonprofits, job sites, churches; institutional spaces such as county government offices; and business spaces such as plant facilities, union meetings, and so forth. Diagram 1.3 illustrates the complexities of this niche, but these complexities are different from social services and education programs. That is, the approaches required of staff in economic development nonprofits are typically not direct service work, lessening staff exposure to the stress and trauma of people being served.

The advocacy and reform services and programs niche is easier to identify in the nonprofit landscape. As readers likely notice, the social services and education niches can be experienced by staff, and the populations being served, as concentric circles with varying degrees of overlap. Readers can also imagine the overlap of specialized programs where social services and economic development programs make sense to be closely collaborating. However, most often, economic development programs and the professionals who run them rarely engage in direct services. This is also common among the advocacy and reform programs niche. Advocacy and reform programs involve populations at a distance in terms of research, writing, speaking, and activating and elevating the public's voice. Advocacy and reform programs are not direct services like in the case of social services and education programs. The people served by advocacy and reform programs include folks across the lifespan as well as animals and the environment; these are services and programs that push for and design solutions to system barriers and institutional oppression.

The approaches used by these nonprofit staff members—research, writing, speaking, and elevating the public's voice—unfold in a few contexts, including the offices of nonprofits, community sites where targeted gatherings are coordinated, governmental offices, and digital spaces such as social media and news media outlets. Sometimes these nonprofit staff can be compared to those working in direct services with traumatized populations. For example, secondary exposure to stress and trauma

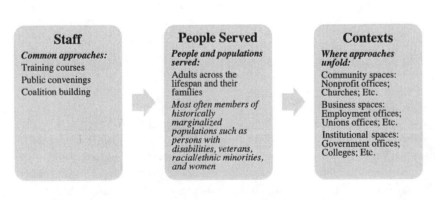

Diagram 1.3 Economic development services and programs in nonprofit community-based organizations.

is shown to happen in terms of *secondary trauma*, also sometimes called *contagious trauma*, where the professionals must study information about the suffering and injustices of populations that they are working (Coddington, 2017). It is important to understand that this secondary trauma can impact these professionals through the course of reading documents and interviewing members of the populations though these routes of taking on stress and trauma of the people being served is not usually as deep and prolonged as it is for professionals in social services programming (Knuckey, Satterthwaite & Brown, 2018). Diagram 1.4 illustrates the complexities of this niche.

Arts and culture services and programs are another niche within the nonprofit sector and this niche, like all of the niches, is complex. The diversity of job roles includes several types of modalities across various program goals. The people served within this services and program niche vary greatly: children and teens, elders and young families, marginalized youth and symphony membership holders, and so forth. The types of modalities used by professionals serve functions across music, dance, crafts, painting, sculpting, design, and so forth. Still further, the intended outcomes within this services and program niche can include increased skills, knowledge, and access to the arts, but can also involve inventions such as hybrids like mariachi opera (Hagerty, 2018), elevating folk content, and new takes on established artforms (e.g., trans portraits).

Diagram 1.5 illustrates some of the intricacies of this niche, and similar to social services, the approaches required of staff teams can create some amount of exposure to stress and trauma depending on the demographics, modalities, and intended goals of serving specific populations. For example, some modalities bring staff and program participants into close proximity and other modalities less so (e.g., online/remote design).

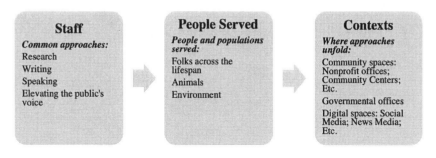

Diagram 1.4 Advocacy and reform services and programs in nonprofit community-based organizations.

The close proximity between staff and traumatized and oppressed popula-tions—which is a hallmark of nonprofit community-based social services work—can show up here in the arts and culture realm when serving, for instance, children with regularly occurring art therapy classes at a domes-tic violence shelter.

The environment services and programs niche includes activities that sometimes involve direct services. For example, trainings on the risks and detriments associated with invasive species are often provided in class-room settings or through social media. Such trainings target populations who can be unintentionally involved in the transport of invasive species, including folks such as interstate fishermen and practicing shamans with animal components to their rituals. Similar to advocacy and reform pro-grams, nonprofits focused on environment services and programs serve populations in terms of trainings, writings, and fieldwork research. Train-ings, writings, and research are for the purposes of triaging imminent threats and long-term solution-building around environmental issues. The approaches used in environment services and programs typically distance

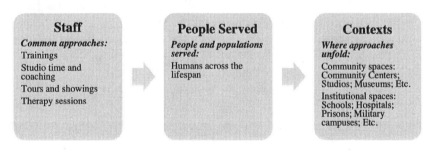

Diagram 1.5 Arts and culture services and programs in nonprofit community-based organizations.

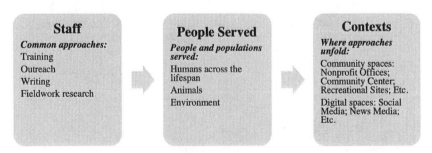

Diagram 1.6 Environment services and programs in nonprofit community-based organizations.

staff teams from directly partnering with traumatized people. Hence, chronic stress and vicarious trauma among these nonprofit professionals is minimal compared to those working in direct services programs, programs that are 100 percent about direct services. Diagram 1.6 illustrates the interplay between staff approaches for delivering the services and programs in this niche, the people and environment engaged, and the contextual settings that include community and digital spaces.

Those professionals and job roles encompassed under the emergency response services and program niche includes direct services in the same human-to-human connection manner as those in the social services niche. However, emergency response services are separated in this chapter from social services because of, first, the focus of these professionals and, second, the short-term intention of the services and programs. The focus of such services and programs is typically assessing and triaging injuries as well as eminent threats. These nonprofit professionals use medical and mental health tools and tactics for carrying a population from threat to a state of stability where then nonprofit community-based social services and education niches pick up the long-term service needs. For example, following a police shooting of a Black or Brown community member, an emergency response program might include neighborhood responders trained in peer-to-peer "mental health first aid" to triage the immediate trauma experienced by the family of the shooting victim and the neighbors (Morgan et al., 2018).

Another example of emergency response services and programs includes coordinating immediate food transport to neighborhoods or cities negatively impacted by a natural disaster such as Hurricane Katrina in 2005 and the coronavirus pandemic in 2019–2021. Similar to the direct services found in the social services and education niches, staff working in the context of emergency response must come close to the stress and trauma of populations in order to effectively fulfill their job descriptions. Hence, there is almost no distance between the staff teams and the populations served. Many studies show that working in emergency response jobs—nonprofit and governmental such as the national guard—is similar to the chronic stress and vicarious trauma that the nonprofit community-based social services professionals experience who are centered in this book (Shakespeare-Finch and Daley, 2017; Shakespeare-Finch et al., 2015).

The job role overlap that is experienced by nonprofit professionals in social services and emergency response niches is multifaceted and extremely relevant with regard to the coronavirus pandemic. For example, many who have full-time positions in nonprofit community-based social services organizations became emergency responders to ensure that historically marginalized communities as well as hospital staff had access to food, temporary housing, and childcare in the context of governmental orders to close schools, companies, and public spaces across the U.S.

In 2020, lack of access to food, temporary housing, and childcare in the U.S. occurred in relation to public health requirements focused on decreasing population exposure to the coronavirus. Also, the public health expectation for mitigating population exposure to the coronavirus included encouraging self-quarantine for elder volunteers. Dangerously, many places across the U.S. have relied on volunteers in retirement years to transport food from designated supplier sites such as grocery stores to food pantries where community members can shop for themselves and their families. With minimal transport volunteers, such a food system nearly halts. Social services professionals and younger volunteers were seen stepping up at an urgent pace to get food to pantries. My own weekly contribution as a grocery store "gleaner" is such an example. Still further, with the coronavirus public health expectations of 10 feet of space between beds in temporary housing, housing facilities moved some of their operations to hotels. Nonprofit community-based social services professionals transitioned into 24/7 providers in order to support hotel housing while keeping their fingers crossed, badly needing volunteers with the appropriate skill set to step in.

Further, the emergency response niche is typically only conceived of as professionals with official job titles, but historically there are informal, grassroots groups and networks that meet the needs of the most marginalized. Getting food and baby formula to families today, rent money to laid-off workers tomorrow, and childcare to working parents is quickly addressed by grassroots networks. That is, the individuals who comprise these networks—church-based or otherwise—can identify the people, their needs, and resources to meet those needs because they carry historical knowledge and networks. It is not their career roles; it is their social, familial, and religious roles that allow them to act as emergency responders. *Does Ms. Rogers have groceries for the week? No? Then by 6 p.m. at night someone will knock on her front door and hand her a bag of groceries.*

The formalizing of emergency responders in this niche such as the Red Cross and clinicians is important, but it is important to recognize that the work that gets done in this niche is heavily supported by the informal responders. The history of this niche is based on the informal networks of people looking after people who are sometimes professionals in nonprofits

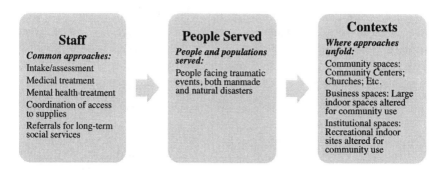

Diagram 1.7 Emergency response services and programs in nonprofit community-based organizations.

and other times members of a church or neighborhood where collective action is part of the history of our survival. We see this more so in times of panic.

Ultimately, in the emergency response niche, the roles that professionals take on bring them into close proximity to high-stress scenarios, with stressed and often traumatized people. Their use of intake assessments, medical and mental health treatments, coordination of access to needed supplies, and referrals to long-term social services with other organizations are the approaches that are needed for the community being served but are also the mechanism for the ways that chronic stress and vicarious trauma occur among these professionals. Diagram 1.7 illustrates the interplay between their approaches for delivering the services and programs, the populations who are engaged, and the contextual settings where emergency responses typically unfold.

Proximity Links Professionals to Chronic Stress and Vicarious Trauma

While nonprofit community-based organizations are led by the executive leadership, including the Chief Executive Officer or Executive Director and the Board of Directors, these roles do not include the implementation of services and programs. The executive leadership focuses their time and talent on strategy and funding to keep the organization's doors open ... well, this is the theoretical focus. Some nonprofits do have, in reality, executive leadership who inform or serve in direct service capacities, but that's another story for another time.

41

As was outlined in the above discussion of each of the services and program niches, the implementers of services and programs are the direct service professionals and their managers. They use their years of specialized know-how, formal training, and lived experiences to determine when, how, and where community members are engaged. Specifically:

1. These staff members determine *the when* by determining whether persons are eligible for services and programs and/or the level of threat persons face due to systemic barriers.
2. These staff members design *the how* by way of the approaches discussed in detail earlier such as with the approaches listed in the earlier Diagrams 1.1 to 1.7. Nonprofit community-based social services professionals use approaches that bring them close to the human experiences of trauma and oppression.
3. These staff members determine *the where*, prioritizing the most accessible locations such as within homes or churches, schools or community centers, and so forth.

These talented, on-the-ground professionals are central to the workings of the nonprofit sector. While they, ironically, have the least amount of say in the strategies and fundraising that consume the executive leaders, they make the sector exist as a "force for good" (Crutchfield & Grant, 2012).

Examples of *the when, how,* and *where* were subtly presented in the Introduction of this book when readers met Lee and Alice, direct service professionals. Lee selected which community sites and neighborhoods, on which days, and during which times of day he visited families facing homelessness. Bridging families to temporary housing with the aim of eventual access to long-term housing, required Lee to use his professional know-how, formal training, and lived experiences to determine *the when, how,* and *where* within the scope of his job role. His skills emerged seamlessly, allowing him to effectively deliver on his position description, posi-tively impact people, and keep himself safe in contexts where this may be a challenging expectation. Importantly, there is a duality that must be highlighted; this duality leads us to the core of the problem that this book takes on:

> *Proximity Matters*
>
> *Lee's professional know-how, formal training, and lived experiences can never prevent exposure to the stress and trauma experienced by the people he serves since close proximity is integral to performing his job.*

Lee's professional know-how, formal training, and lived experiences are the glue that make nonprofit community-based social services possible for responding to social inequities. Yet, his professional know-how, formal training, and lived experiences can never prevent exposure to the stress and trauma experienced by the people he serves since close proximity is integral to performing his job. Hence, chronic stress and vicarious trauma are integral to Lee's job.

Lee's talent, like the talent of all social services professionals and their managers, cannot stop chronic stress and vicarious trauma. Mitigating the negative impact of chronic stress and vicarious trauma is not an individual talent to cultivate. Mitigating the negative impact relies on the interplay of individual, organizational and sector level tools and commitments discussed in the latter chapters of this book.

Closing

As readers already understand, it is nonprofit community-based social services professionals who engage in doing direct service work who are featured in this book. They are the force that moves the nonprofit sector's responses to social inequities and yet they are treated as the most expendable. Describing the work context for nonprofit community-based social services jobs in this chapter introduces readers to the chronic stress and vicarious trauma that is woven into the line items of the job descriptions, the hiring contracts, and the seemingly ordinary expectations placed on these professionals. Chronic stress and vicarious trauma are central to the very fulfillment of job expectations and required service delivery approaches.

Comparing and contrasting nonprofit community-based social services experiences with experiences in services and programs in the other niches—education, economic development, advocacy and reform, arts and culture, environment, and emergency response—provides details and insights about the factors involved in the ways that chronic stress and vicarious trauma occur. And two factors are the most important for understanding what's killin' nonprofit community-based social services professionals. First, services and programs unfold through *direct contact* with stressed and traumatized people from communities who are historically oppressed. Second, services and programs unfold across *long periods* where professionals spend significant amounts of time with stressed and traumatized people, again, from communities who are historically oppressed.

Nonprofit community-based social services jobs will always involve chronic stress and vicarious trauma. The purpose of this profession is to resolve social inequities by directly engaging marginalized populations, attempting to triage and transform the shared historical trauma of racism, sexism, classism, homophobia, and xenophobia that infiltrates American families and individuals. It is true that direct service roles do exist in various niches and not just nonprofit community-based social services careers as was discussed earlier in this chapter. For example, in the arts and culture services and program niche, art therapy programs that serve combat veterans bring staff and the population into *close proximity*, where stress and trauma of the population permeate into the bodies and minds of the professionals. However, in many niches across the nonprofit sector, greater distance exists between nonprofit professionals and the populations who they serve than it does for the Lees and Alices in the sector.

In fact, Diagrams 1.1 to 1.7 illustrate the linkages among professional approaches, people and populations served, and settings where services and programs unfold. These linkages make it simple to understand the ways that certain types of nonprofit jobs, specifically social services jobs, involve close contact with specific groups of people in order to make a positive transformation. These linkages are further explored in the next chapter, but the landscaping function of this chapter provides discussion of the major niches and job types, setting up readers to walk confidently into further discussion elsewhere in this book. Whether you, the reader, are already a nonprofit community-based social services professional or considering a career in this sector, this chapter gave you the groundwork to understand the who, what, where, when, and how of nonprofit organizations, social services nonprofit jobs, and the badass professionals who serve on the front lines of social change.

CHAPTER 2

How Exposure Happens

Nonprofit community-based social services professionals are exposed to stress and trauma that are carried by the community members who they serve. In the course of fulfilling the line items on their job descriptions, these professionals vicariously experience the barriers and oppressions that the community members do. In this chapter, let's look at the ways that this happens in community-based nonprofit organizations by exploring a survey study and the lives of four professionals.

All of those who are delivering social services to stressed and traumatized individuals and families must contend with the chronic stress and vicarious trauma involved in providing thoughtful, proven, and strategic resources to those who benefit from them. To do this successfully, building authentic relationships with traumatized persons is required and these relationships expose professionals to chronic stress and vicarious trauma. Notice that these experiences are rarely listed in the job announcements.

In your reading of this chapter, four nonprofit community-based social services professionals in community-based organizations illustrate five dynamics common among those who serve in direct service job roles. These are jobs that are geared to directly partner with people from diverse and frequently oppressive walks of life. The five dynamics include the following:

1. Working with suffering persons and seeing their obvious suffering creates chronic stress and vicarious trauma.
2. Being a victim of a crime or an attempted crime by a person being served or someone else in the service setting creates chronic stress and event-specific trauma.
3. Moving through unsafe spaces like violent crime neighborhoods creates chronic stress.
4. Serving on-call for emergency situations such as help hotlines or local crises creates chronic stress and vicarious trauma.

5. Working long hours, with limited resources, with the constant worry about the well-being of community members being served creates chronic stress.

These five dynamics are explored in detail with Alex, Tania, Maribel, and Richard in order to accomplish two things. First, nonprofit community-based social services professionals reading this book can see themselves, their colleagues, and their clients in the stories. This may very well be the first time that such professionals witness themselves as center state in conversations about job-based chronic stress and vicarious trauma.

Second, those who love direct service staff such as spouses, siblings, neighbors, and collaborators benefit from understanding the very brilliance of these professionals; their brilliance shines even in the midst of straining circumstances. They get resources to the right people, creatively, and at great cost to their health. The four professionals featured in this chapter share their experiences of chronic stress and vicarious trauma in ways that reflect the variation in work settings, job titles, and service approaches. These examples move us deep into the specific niche of nonprofit social services, helping us to understand the ways that job exposure to chronic stress and vicarious trauma unfold. By the end of this chapter, through the discussion of the survey study and the experiences of Alex, Tania, Maribel, and Richard, readers get to see the ingenuity, willingness, and suffering of nonprofit, community-based social services professionals.

How Far Does the Problem Reach?

At the end of 2018, through my role at California State University, Fresno, I conducted a survey study on the exposure of nonprofit community-based social services professionals in community-based organizations to chronic stress and vicarious trauma. While many studies exist on the exposure of social workers, medical professionals, and relief personnel, none previously existed with a sole focus on nonprofit staff in social service and direct service jobs. The survey study captured the experiences of professionals across urban and rural sites in 12 U.S. states and one international site. The study found that many nonprofit professionals who are working directly with clients are experiencing chronic stress and vicarious trauma through the course of fulfilling their roles with community members. Below are the descriptors of the survey participants. Overall, 94 professionals responded to the survey though only 87 were currently employed at community-based nonprofits and, further, only 73 were employed full-time. Hence, 73 professionals were the focus of data analysis.

Table 1. Age of survey respondents

Age	Number	%
18–30	19	26%
31–40	21	29%
41–50	15	21%
51–60	8	11%
61–70	10	14%
	73	**100%**

Table 2. Sex of survey respondents

Sex	Number	%
Female	53	73%
Male	20	27%
Intersex	0	0%
Nonbinary	0	0%
	73	**100%**

Table 3. Heritage of survey respondents

Heritage	Number	%
Black	1	1%
Jewish	1	1%
Latino	9	12%
Native American	1	1%
Southeast Asian	1	1%
White	52	71%
Latino and Native American	1	1%
Native American and White	1	1%
Southeast Asian, South Asian, Pacific Islander, Latino	1	1%
South East Asian and Pacific Islander	1	1%
Unidentified	4	5%
	73	**100%**

Table 4. Location of survey respondents

Location (U.S. States)	Number	%
CA	56	77%
MO	2	3%
NY	2	3%
VA	2	3%
DC	1	1%
FL	1	1%
GA	1	1%
IL	1	1%
MI	1	1%
MN	1	1%
NC	1	1%
OH	1	1%

Location (U.S. States)	Number	%
International	1	1%
Unknown	2	3%
	73	100%

Table 5. Years that survey respondents were in community-based nonprofits

Years in community-based nonprofits	Number	%
1 to 2	8	11%
3 to 5	17	23%
6 to 9	17	23%
10 to 15	14	19%
16 to 20	6	8%
21 to 29	7	10%
30+	4	5%
	73	100%

Among the respondents, some maintained managerial and direct services roles, while others engaged in solely direct services with community members. That is, when examining survey responses to prompts about job roles, it is clear that 46 professionals or 63 percent indicated that they had responsibilities that included direct service work, but not as managers, only as supervisees. Below in further discussion on chronic stress and vicarious trauma among the professionals, this distinction will be explored.

The respondents learned about the opportunity to participate in the study through a snowball approach where I sent the electronic survey link and a chance to win one of three $20 Visa gift cards or one of two $50 Visa gift cards. The snowball approach meant that I emailed basic study information to several nonprofit community-based organizations, community foundations, and associations across the U.S.; anyone who received the email could forward the email further to their contacts. The survey software prevented respondents from possibly submitting more than one time.

For this study, chronic stress and vicarious trauma were measured through the use of survey questions from the Copenhagen Burnout Inventory (CBI) (Kristensen et al., 2005) and the Vicarious

Measuring Chronic Stress and Vicarious Trauma

24% of direct service professionals report that, outside of work time, they think about distressing issues faced by the community members who they serve.

48

Trauma Scale (VTS) (Aparicio et al., 2013). The CBI was invented to measure predictors of burnout; burnout is the last stop on the train in terms of chronic stress, compassion fatigue, and vicarious trauma. Those indicators pertaining to chronic stress were borrowed for my study. The VTS was designed for assessing distress levels among professions known to be working with traumatized populations involved in the legal system. Some, but not all, of the vicarious trauma prompts were used from the VTS.

For the purposes of my study, the introduction content for the survey was adjusted from the original CBI and VTS in order to remove leading language (i.e., wording that could lead respondents to answer in a manner that they believed that they were supposed to). The survey study email was framed as focused on questions pertaining to nonprofit jobs generally. The revising of these tools for nonprofit professionals was done to avoid the use of terms like "burnout" and "stress." Also to avoid the possibility of biased responses, possibly leading questions about vicarious trauma were not included in my survey. For example, before the four vicarious trauma indicators listed below, questions that can lead the survey respondents to focus on their jobs as the source of trauma included *My job requires exposure to traumatized or distressed* clients and *My job involved exposure to distressing materials and experiences.* These two survey prompts were not included.

While the CBI and VTS are proven effective in their original forms, the additional layers of precaution were used with nonprofit professionals to prevent survey respondents from unintentionally choosing what they thought were the "right" responses. In order to get as reliable information as possible, these cautious steps were important for my study.

The survey responses among the professionals in direct services roles ranged 15 percent to 52 percent on the chronic stress indicators listed below. For reading the list of 11 chronic stress indicators, a "yes" is based on the professionals responding to the survey prompts with *often or to a high degree* and *always or to a very high degree yes* (i.e., the full set of response options included the following: Always or To a very high degree, Often or To a high degree, Sometimes or somewhat, Seldom or To a low degree, Never/almost never or To a very low degree). For the final prompt in this chronic stress list, a "yes" is derived from the response options *absolutely yes* and *mostly yes* (i.e., the full set of response options included the following: Absolutely Yes, Mostly Yes, Sometimes Yes/No, Mostly No, Absolutely No).

- 24 (52%) confirmed yes for *Do you feel worn out at the end of the working day?*
- 15 (33%) confirmed yes for *Are you exhausted in the morning at the thought of another day at work?*
- 8 (17%) confirmed yes for *Do you feel that every working hour is tiring for you?*
- 60 (72%) confirmed no for *Do you have enough energy for family and friends during leisure time?*
- 22 (48%) confirmed yes for *Outside of work life, do you feel tired?*
- 18 (39%) confirmed yes for *Outside of work life, are you physically exhausted (i.e., your body is tired)?*
- 20 (43%) confirmed yes for *Outside of work life, are you emotionally exhausted (i.e., your mind is tired or your motivation is low)?*
- 13 (28%) confirmed yes for *Outside of work life, do you think: "I can't take it anymore?"*
- 16 (35%) confirmed yes for *Outside of work life, do you feel worn out?*
- 12 (26%) confirmed yes for *Outside of work life, do you feel weak and susceptible to illness?*
- 7 (15%) confirmed yes for *Finally, do you have a mental health issue that is formally or informally diagnosed which is made worse by your work experiences (i.e., informally = you can tell that you have a mental health need, such as depression or anxiety, but a doctor has never diagnosed you)?*

Further, for the 63 percent of professionals who were working directly with members of the community, who were solely supervisees, many of them experienced vicarious trauma; the scores ranged 13 percent to 24 percent on the vicarious trauma indicators listed below. Let's reflect on what the professionals shared about their experiences with these four indicators. Notably for these professionals, 61 percent of them were working more than 40 hours per week in these roles. For the calculations listed below, a "yes" is based on the professionals responding to the survey prompts with *often or to a high degree* and *always or to a very high degree yes* (i.e., the full set of response options included the following: Always or To a very high degree, Often or To a high degree, Sometimes or somewhat, Seldom or To a low degree, Never/almost never or To a very low degree).

- 6 (13%) confirmed yes for *I find myself distressed by listening to my clients' stories and situations.*

- 11 (24%) confirmed yes for *I find myself thinking about distressing client/program participant issues outside of work.*
- 11 (24%) confirmed yes for *Sometimes I feel helpless to assist my clients in the way I would like.*
- 8 (17%) confirmed yes for *Sometimes it is hard to stay positive and optimistic given some of the things I encounter in my work.*

The existence of unmitigated chronic stress and vicarious trauma can seem like an ironic dynamic for working in nonprofit community-based social services settings. That is, the entire purpose of these social services is to supply resources that resolve, heal, and transform oppressive situations. Yet, business as usual in these jobs ensures that unmitigated chronic stress and vicarious trauma drag down professionals and can even impact sector-wide effectiveness. It is clear from the analysis of chronic stress and vicarious trauma indicators above as well as further analysis below that the thoughtful, human-to-human connection required for serving stressed and traumatized populations pulls the professionals into those oppressive situations, casting holograms of oppression in the workplace.

Let's consider more insights from the professionals who responded to the survey study. From 24 of the respondents, we can learn about the types of oppressive situations that they navigate alongside the community members who they serve. The following examples are based on the professionals' responses to the survey prompt *Please quickly share the major challenges or barriers that your clients face that bring them to your nonprofit for services:*

- Poverty, limited English proficiency, need for advocate, direct support services.
- Lack of training. Lack of professional development.
- Needing free counseling for sexual violence experiences, wanting free healthy relationship educational programs, wanting advocacy support for court and hospital appointments relating to sexual violence experiences. Barriers are low-income, low-support, and lack of education in our area.
- We treat and help patients admitted to hospice. I set up volunteers to help the family/caregivers get some respite by providing volunteers. This is a Medicare requirement.
- Lack of education, lack of personal resources, low socioeconomic status, single parent homes.
- Job training, food needs, family crisis.

- Families affected by disability.
- Housing and employment.
- Healthcare needs.
- Job acquisition and skills training.
- Under-resourced areas where our services aren't accessible. Poverty where survival or cultural norms take precedence over wellness.
- Low income, high crime, underserved communities.
- Seeking acceptance as LGBTQ+ people who have been rejected by their families and faith communities.
- Addiction, homelessness, trust.
- Food insecurity.
- Mental health, substance abuse, homeless, unemployed, uneducated, and health and disease management.
- Sex workers. Opportunity youth.
- Racism, language/economic/ immigration status.
- Housing affordability.
- Lack of a good support system at home. Need for tutoring. Many clients come from "broken homes."

> *Understanding Oppression in the Workplace*
>
> *41% of direct service professionals wonder how long they can keep serving community members.*

- Not all members have a stable home life. Most members are low income.
- Youths have placement orders; therefore, they don't have a place to return upon their release and the majority of the population goes to a group home.
- Many of my clients are struggling with housing and transportation. They also struggle with finding work.
- Language barriers, access to transportation, stable housing and employment opportunities.

What about the managers who support these direct service professionals? There were 46 of 73 professionals who solely delivered direct services, nine who solely managed "direct reports," and 18 who supervised including volunteers in some cases, while also providing direct services to community members. The vicarious trauma calculations appeared to be shared among those professionals who were working solely with community members and yet higher for the 18 with time split between managing direct reports and delivering direct services.

52

- 6 (33%) confirmed yes for *I find myself distressed by listening to my clients' stories and situations.*
- 11 (61%) confirmed yes for *I find myself thinking about distressing client/program participant issues outside of work.*
- 11 (61%) confirmed yes for *Sometimes I feel helpless to assist my clients in the way I would like.*
- 8 (44%) confirmed yes for *Sometimes it is hard to stay positive and optimistic given some of the things I encounter in my work.*

There are several research studies that help us to understand the link between chronic stress and vicarious trauma and the quality of services provided to the community. For instance, "compassion fatigue" lowers quality assurance outcomes, indicating that the people who are being served are receiving lower quality services, including the lowering of outcomes surrounding programmatic effectiveness and efficiency (Morrissette, 2016; Timm, 2016). This is not a condemnation of the professionals; rather, discussion of program quality offers a reality check on what happens under the working conditions of unmitigated chronic stress and vicarious trauma. A previously passionate, invested, and talented professional can become unrecognizable to their former self. This reality is troubling to everyone who loves and relies on nonprofit community-based social services.

Many survey respondents also provided examples of what they do to manage their workplace experiences. These efforts span many tactics, but Netflix was a regularly used approach! Below are the voices of 48 professionals who responded to the prompt *Please list what you do to cope or respond to your work experiences:*

- Time with my family is at the top of that list and my religious faith helps me more than anything else.
- Doing something physical or nothing.
- Running, biking, hiking, television.
- Exercise, dog, unplugging, not checking email outside of work.
- Exercise, movies on Netflix or Amazon Prime.
- Beer, hobbies, hot baths.
- Nothing.
- Meditation, exercise (walking), watching sports, writing.
- Therapy, exercise, spiritual direction, prayer/meditation, authentic friendships, activities with my children and family.
- I garden, see my grandchildren, work on DIY projects, attend university plays and cook.

- Counseling, reading, yoga, deep breathing exercises.
- Sleep, watching television, taking a walk, talking with my partner, hobbies, Valium.
- Netflix binges.
- Netflix, reading, sewing, walking.
- Internet binging, drinking copious amounts of soda, taking long walks.
- Running, sports (playing and watching), go for a walk, drink, watch Netflix.
- Reading and watching the NFL on Sundays.
- Time with family and friends, travel when I can, read.
- A beer or wine each day, exercise, hanging out with the family/pets.
- Dance, Netflix, other roles (non-work).
- Pray, read, spend time with husband.
- Netflix binging or often catching a nap after work.
- Acupuncture and massage therapy, exercise, Netflix binges.
- Time with friends and family, yoga.
- I spend time hanging out with my teenage daughter. I love to go to the movies or read a good book and get lost in a good story.
- Netflix, other videos/shows, arts and crafts, play with kitties.
- Spend time with friends and family. Sometimes nap on weekends. Walk my dog. Play games.
- Exercise, Netflix binges, venting to close friends (but you have to be careful, because you don't want to speak poorly of your organization).
- Exercise, spend time with family.
- Pray and Hallmark movies.
- Communication with friends, quality time with spouse and children, cooking and cleaning. Occasional Netflix binges/random internet or social media scrolling.
- Drinking, watching tv/movies, and exercise.
- Baking, exercising.
- Wine, talking about it with my spouse, hot yoga.
- Exercise, daily glass of wine, going outside (to the mountains) on the weekends without exception.
- Occasional wine, venting to friends, exercise.
- Exercise.
- I play with my daughter (I have a four-year-old).
- Netflix, traveling, self-care.

- Going on walks, spending time with my family, prayer … talking to my husband.
- Faith-based, Perspective, clear boundaries, supportive family.
- Smoking a blunt, whiskey and Netflix comedies
- Prayer, retreats, reading, walking, playing with my dogs, drives in the country and mtns with my spouse.
- Word puzzles, phone, Pokémon; phone, shop amazon, water grass/ flowers, FB/social media, walk, play with kids, clean my house, have a beer.
- Exercise, Netflix binges, Hulu shows, shopping, playing with my dogs, listening to music.
- Play games and sometimes I do creative projects.
- Reading, movies, family time, naps.
- Nothing.
- Starbucks coffee every morning, prayers, Netflix binges with my kids on weekends, Scrabble with my husband Sunday evenings, naps whenever possible, read magazines whenever possible.
- Therapy, one on one sessions with spiritual Director or life coach, daily meditation, gardening, 28:1 ratio CBD tincture.
- Netflix binges, spa days, working from home in my PJs, date nights (movies & live music events), singing with a women's group and with a band.
- Spending time with friends and my husband.
- Speaking with my supervisor, who is also my mentor and a close personal friend with similar experiences. Spending time with my wife and dogs, hiking, movies, visiting my parents and playing video games.
- Daily evening walks (20–30 minutes).
- Therapy, decompress with friends, mindless phone games on the commute home, stay home from protests or other draining activism, loudly tell everyone I know that non-profits are just a feel-good tax shelter for the rich and will never achieve true systemic change.
- Netflix, meet with friends, go outdoors.
- Dark chocolate candy at night after I put my daughter to bed while watching an episode of a show on Netflix.
- Singing in a band, crafting, playing guitar, watching movies/TV, time with family and friends.
- Prayer, family interactions, church activities, vigorous walks with our dogs and/or my sons.

- Not much, sometimes Netflix binges.
- Gym, music and watching Food Network and wrestling.
- Netflix binges, reading novels, walking my dog, exercising.
- Play with my kids, play games on my phone/tablet, read books, watch sports on TV.
- Meditation, yoga, biking, devotional reading, motivational reading, play with pets, walking, intentional daydreaming, writing.
- Wine, binge eating, vacation.
- Go on walks with my homeboy (dog) and watch movies.
- time with my honey, his emotional support is important. Occasionally a day requires a glass of wine or two.
- I laugh a lot by watching funny shows, will read books, or spend time with my dogs.
- Enjoy time with my children, talking to them about their school day and watching their favorite TV shows.
- Wine, reading, watch tv with my husband.
- Talk with friends and colleagues.
- Wine/beer with dinner, playing with my animals, yoga/ meditation, working out.

In the context of unmitigated chronic stress and vicarious trauma throughout the nonprofit community-based social services niche, eventual burnout seems likely for many of those who responded to the survey study. Remember that burnout is the experience of physical and psychological fatigue from undertaking roles and tasks that are beyond the scope of the individual's ability and/or beyond the scope of institutional support for the roles and tasks to be accomplished (Lu et al., 2016). Burnout can be predicted for a population based on the levels of chronic stress and vicarious trauma that are present among the population. In fact, an employment survey that scanned the nonprofit sector reported that 45 percent of nonprofit professionals, beyond the social services niche, were already reporting or were at risk of burnout (Word et al., 2011). Additional studies that are relevant to exploring the work climate in the nonprofit sector show that without structural changes to the work context to mitigate experiences like chronic stress, burnout is almost certain (Baines et al., 2002; Kanter & Sherman, 2017).

While my survey study results focus on nonprofit community-based social services professionals with special attention to those in direct service roles, the results largely reflect what has been found across the nonprofit sector. However, of special interest for understanding the social service niche and direct service professionals, a portion of them have made their suffering clear for the first time through this study. In their responses to three additional survey prompts, we can hear them loud and clear. When asked directly *Does it drain your energy to work with clients/ program participants?* Twenty or 43 percent of direct service respondents confirmed "yes." Further, when asked directly *Are you tired of working with clients/program participants?,* nine or 20 percent confirmed "yes." And, when asked directly *Do you sometimes wonder how long you will be able to continue working with clients/program participants?,* 19 or 41 percent confirmed "yes."

The professionals also provided examples of what their nonprofit community-based organizations could do to mitigate their workplace experience. The details of these recommendations are important to consider. Equally important to consider is the rate at which ideas were put forth, suggesting a desire by professionals for some type of organizational solution. Hearing their voices matters; this book is about how nonprofits are killing these professionals. Below are the voices of 46 professionals, responding to the prompt *Finally, please share any ways that you wish that your current organization would support you and/or colleagues with the work-related challenges pertaining to working with clients and/or direct reports:*

- Organizations should offer better ways for caring for employees to deal with the high stress work environments such as therapy, wellness opportunities and more.
- I wish that we were encouraged to take time off now and then without being made to feel guilty.
- Additional support staff. Aware of time constraints before adding additional programs and responsibilities.
- Holding Self Care Seminars or providing opportunities for team-building.
- More realistic expectations.
- Biggest problem is being understaffed for current client demands.
- Health benefits, resources on dealing with high stress situations, conferences, etc.
- Further professional development, supportive programs, better health insurance to pursue treatment for persistent mental illness, increased lines of communication, improvement of agency culture, recognizing that these systemic problems are not just "part of the territory."

- Self-care in the office, more open culture for discussion and critique, minimizing outreach events to advertise services we are backed up in providing.
- I don't particularly suffer from the experiences in this survey, but a more flexible work day would be a great thing for more nonprofits to consider. It's almost never the case that 9–5 is the best hours for us.
- More incentives for pay raise.
- More trust in the work we do, better communication of expectations, leaving work for working hours only.
- There is some issue with communication that makes it challenging to get all the right information, which makes it that much more frustrating for our clients.
- I run many programs, but only have two direct reports. One very PT, the other runs a very tiring/time consuming portion of our org but I feel this person isn't really right for the position anymore and a Board that has a lot of suggestions and ideas but they never follow through leaving me frustrated and tired doing it all myself.
- The organization is mindful and speaks of self-care, but oftentimes still doesn't think through how its action by leadership affect everyone including my direct report.
- While I feel supported by my organization, my long hours are causing burnout. I need healthier boundaries. Another paid staff position would help alleviate the work load.
- Our small staff sometimes leads to too much on everyone's plate and no time to support one another, but I don't know how to fix that.
- Clear job roles, proper accountability, consistent rules applied to all personnel, any communication.
- I would like to be included in the decision-making team. Positive feedback would be nice.
- Less micromanagement and more creativity.
- Aiming to stick to a 40-hour work week as opposed to the 45–50 hours often happening would be great. Encouraging regular breaks—walking outdoors, taking a full lunch hour, etc., would be helpful as well.
- Opportunity for walking, balancing work schedule.
- More autonomy and flex schedule.
- Some counseling services available.
- Suggestion box.
- Colleagues who collaborate on similar issues.

- More authority to reward/promote direct reports.
- Connecting with other nonprofits to address the bigger problems … as there are lots of nonprofits, and we often work with different parts of the puzzle, but rarely collaborate.
- I am very lucky to work for an org which does understand and makes every effort to ensure self-care including a monthly wellness stipend to spend on a massage or therapy, or an ⅛ weed!
- To work more as a complete team instead of everyone being in their silos of responsibility with no regard for others needs or the need for flexibility. Stop being so critical and stop the constant complaining and instead work together to find solutions. The toxic gossip is killing me.
- Raise in pay, more time out of the office, time off, too many events all at once.
- I would like my org to empower staff to take breaks and allow staff to use sick days for mental health breaks as well.
- Weekly or monthly massages.
- More resources for both staff and client needs.
- Provide our department with more staff.
- Ask/implement short staff survey to assess how staff are feeling and implement changes based on findings.
- Down time.
- More collaborative communication and support among the entire agency. Ensuring that employees are all on the same page when new policies and procedures are implemented. Being more available for issues that arise. Being more open-minded and less discriminating.
- Hiring one to two more staff members to assist with the work load. As well as offering competitive pay.
- More training on how to deal with stress at work.
- My organization already does a lot to support me and my colleagues: biannual retreats, monthly learning cohorts, periodic team outings for team-building, book studies together.
- I wish the Board would take greater interest in understanding the day to day.
- I think having a more engaged CEO would be helpful for our organization. Our CEO seems to be disconnected from the work the line staff do with clients and doesn't seem to understand the work that goes in to managing our caseloads.
- More time off and more help so that everyone wouldn't end up working 80+ hours per week.

- Covering cost of exercise classes, massages, child care support.
- Leadership needs to stop trying to grow just for the sake of growing, and focus more on local issues. Exec Director does not listen to staff nor care about their issues (nor does the board of directors for that matter).

Thank You for Making This Your Career

Earlier in this book, Lee and Alice provided examples for readers to chew on about the everyday grind of their work lives. Their examples illustrated the interconnectedness of serving stressed and traumatized populations and experiencing job-based chronic stress and vicarious trauma. Their examples are important, but their examples did not allow insights into the ways that jobs tasks, one at a time, induce chronic stress and/or vicarious trauma. For that reason, Alex, Tania, Maribel, and Richard invite us into their work lives for further understanding.

Alex

Alex is in her 40s and has worked in positive youth development programs for over 15 years. She came to this work from her previous role as a teaching assistant at an elementary school in the same city. Her commitment to this work is firm; she is adamant about getting youth who are living in inner-city, under-resourced neighborhoods relevant services and programs. Alex has a strong reputation for kindness, being down for the long haul, and having contagious laughter. Yet, underneath her reputation, she can't seem to fall asleep and stay asleep, and sleep more than a few hours each night. She even struggles to pay her humble apartment rent on her salary which remains below the sector and geographic medium. Importantly, Alex does not yet have individual tools nor organizational supports to navigate chronic stress and vicarious

> *Serving and Suffering*
>
> *Professionals serving in the nonprofit community-based social services niche get stuck in a vortex of serving and suffering through their dedication to the job, organization, and/or community members.*
>
> *This is coupled with nonprofit sector norms and myths, where this dedication keeps the professional's attention away from their own physiological suffering and/or that the situation is left unmitigated by their organization.*

trauma. Alex faces navigating a vortex of spinning winds, serving young people while suffering under unmitigated chronic stress and vicarious trauma (Schroder et al., 2017). Her sleeping issues, her health, are known only by a few people since such talk might shine a negative light on her employer; she maintains unquestioning loyalty to her nonprofit community-based organization and plans to remain with it for an undetermined period of time even with the current pay and trauma.

Alex is incredibly reflective about how to best serve the young people in her program; her program focuses on sexual health and identity development with teens. She implements the latest research-backed curriculums; gets creative with how to use incentives to recruit program enrollees; attends one to two regional trainings each year to sharpen her insights; and she speaks with everyone about the youth as if they're her own children. Alex has two of her own children who are grown young adults who she raised on this minimal income within the nonprofit community-based social services niche.

No one questions Alex's commitment to the nonprofit sector and to the young people in her program. Not even Alex herself. Her physical suffering such as the sleeping issues and chronic fatigue are personalized in her own interpretation of her well-being. She sees the physical manifestations of stress and vicarious trauma (i.e., unable to sleep) as just things that she is individually experiencing. She does not speak about the link between coaching youth through intimate relationship violence, homelessness, and teen parenthood challenges and her own biological suffering. Because she keeps professional boundaries with the teens, because she is a high performing professional, she conceptually underestimates how their stress and trauma impact her.

In a lot of ways, it would seem insane to tag her job experiences and her health as creating suffering in her life. That is, Alex's parents did not have the privilege to work in their passion area, serving a population less fortunate than themselves, and with a steady paycheck. Alex's parents represented a more obviously oppressed population who worked multiple, hard-labor jobs and when they weren't working, their bodies were drained and in pain. Many in Alex's generation who are working in the social service niche share her generational employment paradigm where their parents had no choice in the matter and so nonprofit sector jobs look like opportunities for living out an ideal career. This assumed ideal is framed as a privilege that their parents couldn't access.

When Alex is coaching young people through intimate relationship violence, homelessness, and teen parenthood challenges, she is subtly screening them to figure out at which point she must act on mandated reporting requirements and/or when to offer more intensive services. For example, when a youth discloses abuse that they experience or that they perpetrate on another, Alex is required by law to report this immediately. Because this type of information often unfolds in a gradual manner through the course of the strong rapport that she builds with the youth, Alex constantly has at the back of her mind a screening process, a vigilance, where she quickly identifies direct and subtle cues that could reveal instances of violence. Her experience has allowed her to carefully track these possibilities and then act as required by law. She accomplishes all of this while also maintaining trust among the entire group of youth who come to know one another through program activities; the youth know that Alex would only report information to the authorities if she absolutely had to.

For example, Alex is not surprised when she learns about intimate relationship violence from a specific young woman. Some of her youth clients tell her directly such as in the case of a 15-year-old young woman who reported to Alex that she loves her boyfriend very much but he hits her in the back of the head and legs if she resists performing oral sex. Even studies show that such violence is more common among teens than among adults, hence Alex's lack of surprise (Taylor & Mumford, 2016) and even more so among LGBTQ youth than CIS youth (Greene et al., 2014; Espelage et al., 2018). Other direct reporting to Alex comes in the forms of writing when Alex is facilitating writing projects with groups of youth. For example, every month, young men like one 17-year-old writes responses to Alex's prompts. The young man writes openly about how annoying his girlfriend is that she cries after sex "like she didn't enjoy it."

Alex is not only providing a research-backed positive youth development program to get developmental supports to these young people, but she is also extending herself to identify safety risks among the youth population. Alex carefully fullfills her responsibilities to build rapport, report crimes, and deliver substantial services. Importantly, many of the youth perpetrating violence among their peers do not recognize their violence as crimes and Alex navigates this tremendously well.

Further, when she picks up on indicators of homelessness, Alex acts quickly. Many youths do not want her to know that they are facing homelessness or do not consider themselves as such. Sleeping on another person's couch—or "doubling up"—is often overlooked for the serious situation that it is (Page, 2017). For example, youth in a doubling up situation are at greatest risk for academic failure (Curry et al., 2020). In other cases of homelessness,

Chapter 2. How Exposure Happens

Alex notices when some of the youth have particularly dirty clothing and hair. She figures out ways to inquire without shaming and offers toiletries and laundry options in the subtlest of ways for the immediate resolving of these issues. Alex is truly artistic in her methods for meeting the immediate hygiene issues of these youth. Alex also stays up to date with youth homeless services in her region, knowing the opening hours, open slots, and criteria for getting any of her program youth into youth homeless shelters. In fact, when she stays late at her office, it is typically because she is securing a resource for a youth, a resource for that very evening.

Because of the needs that emerged over the years, Alex got special permission from her organization's executive leaders to serve the subpopulation of youth in her program that are also teen parents. In this way, she runs a support group for teen moms and a second group for teen dads. These are opportunities for tailored, research-backed services for teen parenthood that include the challenges that come with parenting while still maturing into adulthood.

Alex's job title and description has never changed; she is the "program manager" of the youth program. Though a "program manager," in reality, Alex serves as the outreach specialist, case manager, quasi-therapist, and workshop facilitator. It is important to understand that even though she sounds amazing to non-nonprofit readers, she is the norm in the nonprofit community-based social services niche, a niche full of truly talented professionals. While the daily norms of her social services role require exposure to the stress and trauma of the youth that she serves, no one in her context speaks about the fact that the chronic stress and vicarious trauma is left unmitigated.

Alex's inability to fall and stay asleep at night creates a constant exhaustion in her life. A few hours of sleep per night is bookended between not being able to turn off the "mind chatter" as she calls it and the worries about the youth that occupy a significant portion of her mental space. This "tired and wired" experience is well documented (Wilkins, 2016). Importantly, Alex demonstrates a great degree of professional creativity and solutions for expanding the developmental possibilities of the youth in her program, but she does not apply this growth mindset onto her own well-being, neglecting to understand that she can individually access some of the necessary tools required to improve her well-being. And certainly, she does not apply this growth mindset to her organization as she would see that as unfairly criticizing an organization that does so much for the community. Instead, Alex blames her body and perceived psychological frailty for the sleeplessness, the constant adrenalin rushes, and the frequent worry about the teens. She is like many Americans, however, who individualize the widespread experience of job-related physical illness (Abbas & Raja, 2015; Huyghebaert et al., 2018). The missing ingredient in her understanding of the chronic stress and vicarious trauma is the role of nonprofit cultural beliefs inside her organization and the sector which have become the water in which she swims. The structural oppression faced by most of the youth in her program is projected into her job role, becoming oppression of her own mind and body through the unmitigated chronic stress and vicarious trauma.

Tania

Unlike Alex, Tania is very much aware of the links between serving men who are leaving prison and her difficulties with sleep—falling and staying asleep—as well as what she articulates as "anxiety." That is, her body always feels like she's on "a high," vibrating and her mind is frequently full of jumbled thoughts. Tania cares very much about the people she serves and ensuring that they get a chance to succeed in the community, but she understands that the institutional structure of parole and the barriers to accessing resources guarantees that the majority of these men, who she cares so much about, will be reincarcerated within the year. She takes on every day as if she is at war against structural injustices that will overcome the clients if she lets up in the slightest.

Tania came to this work knowing many people in her family and neighborhood who were incarcerated on and off throughout her life. Now in her late 20s, she is truly happy to have a job where she gets paid to do something that she cares deeply about; Tania can't imagine being in a job that she didn't feel like she had a reason to go to war on each day. Each morning, she arrives at the community center, where her office is located, ready to deplete her mental and physical energy to potentially make a life altering difference in someone's day.

She is quiet, humble, and almost unnoticed in large groups. This makes her a great professional for partnering with the often-timid men who are leaving prison; the men that she works with are most often apprehensive about receiving help, fearful of failure, and nervous about engaging in spaces and places that have changed so much since they were imprisoned years prior. Hence, Tania's fiery passion makes her a great program coordinator to do a lot with a little (i.e., a small amount of time and resources). And her quiet demeanor makes her easily relatable which is perfect for building one-to-one rapport.

Chapter 2. How Exposure Happens

Tania has frank conversations with her supervisor about the link between her inability to sleep at night due to anxious thoughts and dreams related to her job responsibilities. She also shares about her often spinning mind with jumbled thoughts and riding high on waves of "anxiety." While her supervisor is well meaning, he chalks up her experiences to an individualized psychological problem of Tania's own making. The supervisor recommends not reading too deeply into the client's court cases so she doesn't have to think about their "baggage." He also recommends that she not care too much about the men because of the likelihood that their parole officers will violate them and make her feel like a failure. The supervisor is working in this organization because he cares about justice system reform, but Tania disagrees with his sentiments about how to deliver services to the men and she keeps her head down much of the time. With a few early clock-outs each month that her supervisor approves without resistance, she oscillates between quiet grinding in her job role while also occasional advocating that she needs organizational supports in order to not "burnout."

In three ways, Tania is exposed to the stress and trauma of the people that she is serving which transforms into chronic stress and vicarious trauma for her. First, the stress of the clients to access basic living needs becomes her own chronic stress. She works quickly hour by hour to support each person on her caseload. Her clients rarely return to incarceration because of committing new crimes; Tania is adamant that the world would benefit to know that many of the men recidivate because of the stipulations of parole. Many Americans would fail such stipulations such as breaking curfews, interacting with neighbors who are also on parole, and missing a check-in meeting with parole staff after catching a bus to the other side of the city during the four-hour window for these check-ins (Morgan, 2017; Shelden and Vélez Young, 2021).

She spends so much of her time figuring out strategies for the men in her program to stay in good standing with parole requirements rather than where she wishes to invest her time. For example, she knows that supporting access to safe housing, reliable food sources, job opportunities, and psychological healing are vital to the long-term success of the men. With a caseload of 35 to 45 persons at any one time, even though the grant funded program states that the caseload should remain at 25, she focuses on the men staying in good standing with parole officers. Support services like access to housing is her primary job duty, but the practicalities of her job create constant hindrances for her where she spends hours a day strategizing with the men on how to make a job interview appointment while catching one of the few buses to the other side of town for an appointment check-in with parole officers.

Second, Tania spends very little time in conversation with the men about their previous lives and time in prison since such conversations are not needed and they only come up on the rare occasions that the men initiate such an exchange. She has access to their court and prison release documents for any information needed to tailor services such as counseling, job training, and responding to parole dictates. The reading of details about their crimes, and sometimes their histories that hint at past traumas, becomes an access point for vicarious trauma to show up in her job duties. For example, reading about the men's childhood traumas and seeing a trauma throughline in their lives becomes a means for vicarious trauma to be present in her worktime.

Third, she also experiences vicarious trauma from working in neighborhoods that are not safe for her to remain after nightfall. These neighborhoods have the most affordable housing options for the people that she serves, but these neighborhoods mirror historical race and class barriers such as experiencing "food deserts" and "slum lords." Unfortunately, while violent predators live across all types of neighborhoods, much of the gang violence is channeled into these marginalized spaces. When she visits the neighborhoods to drop off a resource such as bus passes, she is in precarious circumstances. On two instances where she was walking to her car after dark, she experienced lewd harassment from unknown men; in these situations explicit statements were made that threatened her safety and inspired her to run to the safety of her car. After these two experiences, she refused to conduct case management tasks after dark.

The chronic stress and vicarious trauma that Tania experiences is constant and obvious. The chronic stress stems from the expansive caseload and pace that she works to meet serious needs. The vicarious trauma stems from her fulfillment of her job description tasks which include reading court documents about violence and crimes as well as moving in unsafe spaces that prove risky even in daylight. Tania's meta-awareness and her unwillingness to individualize and oversimplify the physiological consequences of her chronic stress and vicarious trauma (e.g., lack of sleep and constant buzz of "anxiety") does not protect her. Her supervisor offers no support and lacks an understanding of organizational options that would benefit Tania and her colleagues who engage in similar job roles. He provides no options for mitigating the chronic stress and vicarious trauma. While Tania sees her personal experiences with ill health as part of a systemic problem, like Alex, Tania is no better off at the current time in terms of the negative impact of her job role on her health.

Maribel

Maribel's client population is less socially shamed than those of Alex and Tania. Professionals working with socially stigmatized populations are shown to experience higher rates of stress and fatigue (Benoit et al., 2015; Phillips et al., 2012). In the case of Maribel, she lucked out in terms of not having this added layer of difficulty to her job responsibilities. She works with combat veterans who are enrolled in college. She coordinates a program reliant primarily on a volunteer staff team which coach college students who are combat veterans. The coaching unfolds with trained volunteers; Maribel designs and conducts the training based on the science on post-traumatic stress (PTS) and college retention studies. She tailors services carefully. The services help the students to navigate social and structural barriers commonly experienced by veterans; access necessary resources; and create socializing spaces that can counter isolation and depressive symptoms. More so than in earlier generations of combat veterans, Maribel and her supervisor see the students often speak openly about their experiences with PTS in one-on-one meetings and in small gatherings with peers.

Maribel's previous 10 years of experience working with adults with disabilities prepared her in many ways for this nonprofit community-based social services job. She knows the science of diverse learning styles; social and structural barriers that they face; and, topping these skills, Maribel is trained in treating clients with upmost dignity. Throughout her 20s she was a caseworker, serving adults with disabilities; she faced many situations where the community members who she served experienced heightened stress and trauma. For example, many women who she served with developmental and physical disabilities experienced higher rates of intimate relationship violence than the average American. Also, many of the women and men with disabilities faced higher than average rates of job

> ### Leaving Doesn't Change the Sector
>
> *A social services professional can switch jobs and find a different arrangement of job responsibilities which may alter the configuration of factors that lead to chronic stress and vicarious trauma. Yet, unmitigated chronic stress and/or vicarious trauma remain a constant in nonprofit community-based social services jobs.*

discrimination (Lindsay & Edwards, 2013; McCarthy et al., 2019). Maribel served the adults daily with a laser focus on how to support them in overcoming systemic challenges and social stigma in the course of seeking help with domestic violence and a living wage job. While Maribel acclimated to the intense experiences faced by the adults with disabilities, in her role with student combat veterans she notices a different constant among this student population, that of combat-related PTS.

Maribel is struck by the willingness of student veterans to talk about their experiences with PTS. Research references this as a newer phenomenon among recent veteran populations (Creech & Misca, 2017; Lehavot et al., 2018). In earlier generations, this was less common. While this may appear like progress in terms of mitigating the negative impact of PTS among veterans, it also creates a work climate where professionals like Maribel are more acutely exposed to vicarious trauma.

In her previous job, the caseload for serving adults with disabilities was overwhelming, certainly contributing to chronic stress, like with Tania. Yet, the real-time traumas faced, such as domestic violence among the women, accounted for the weight of vicarious trauma. Contrasting her past and current nonprofit community-based social services jobs, with the student combat veterans, her workload hours are manageable but the influx of vicarious trauma is more pronounced. That is, Maribel gets to maintain the work hours 9 a.m. to 5 p.m., an unusual thing for the niche in which she works. However, chronic stress and vicarious trauma unfold for her in two ways, that of *reading* and *hearing* about current stress and past trauma. The job responsibilities for Maribel and her team of volunteer coaches include reading and hearing about deployment stressors such as military job roles; current physical and psychological illnesses such as alcoholism and acute depression; and strained relationship and family dynamics. This information is formally gathered in order to ensure that program activities are tailored to the students' real needs. However, similar to the students who she serves, Maribel lives in an ongoing state of hypervigilance and mental exhaustion. She wants to avoid triggering her clients and predict triggers (e.g., fourth of July fireworks); stay vigilant to offering them dignity in every interaction; and worries about their home lives and the family members. She did not predict that her current role would actually make her previous role seem easier in many ways.

Maribel's job changes illustrate a core message of this book: Job-specific responsibilities are the means for which chronic stress and vicarious trauma become constants in the lives of nonprofit community-based social services professionals. A social services professional can switch jobs and find a different arrangement of job responsibilities which may alter the configuration of factors that lead to chronic stress and vicarious trauma, yet chronic stress and/or vicarious trauma remain a constant in many nonprofit community-based social services jobs. Now in her 30s with two small children, Maribel more poignantly understands how her challenges with sleeping, her irritability, and mental fog impact her personality and relationships with her children. Part of the magic in Maribel's work is to listen attentively without making the students feel abnormal or embarrassed about difficulties that they face with PTS. In fact, there is nothing abnormal about PTS as it is a natural biological response to overwhelming degrees of stress (Bremner et al., 2017; Davis et al., 2019).

There are many daily challenges, big and small, that she processes with the students. For example, like challenges that many "returning" college students face, many student veterans have to quickly learn about college culture and activities in order to fit into age-specific contexts; their older ages make them look as if they should already be literate in various college scenarios (Fortney et al., 2016; Albright et al., 2017). Still further, Maribel and her volunteer team have come to learn of the all-too-common experience of the veteran students being faced with stinging questions from faculty and peers about whether they were in combat, whether they know anyone who died, and so forth. Layered on top of this painful faux pas are reoccurring painful experiences. For example, different times in the year can be significant for student combat veterans. Without a trusted relationship with students who she serves, Maribel could not predict these circumstances. For example, during summer courses in July, a few students openly warned her that the sound of fireworks can trigger stressful memories for them and even cause some of them to engage in combat-like behavior on the evening of the fireworks. Anniversaries of deaths—associated with combat or not—also significantly impact the students. For these reasons, along with Maribel's serious and committed approach to her job, she experiences hypervigilance around attempts to mitigate the reoccurring and date-specific painful challenges. She sees that the degree of seriousness that she approaches her job with, resulting in both chronic stress and vicarious trauma, is the least she can take on in the course of serving a population who has sacrificed so much of their own lives and those of their families. However, she shares with her closest friends that her job role is not sustainable for her health and family life.

Richard

Richard's title is "outreach specialist" and his job encompasses marketing, canvassing, and helping community members to enroll in government-funded food support which is referred to as "SNAP," Supplemental Nutrition Assistance Program. Readers might be familiar with SNAP under its old name, referred to in past generations as "food stamps." He works for the local food bank which operates this food access program for the local county government. In two ways he experiences chronic stress and vicarious trauma. First, he spends three days a week canvassing very poor neighborhoods, the majority of which are full of people facing tremendous chronic stress themselves. Second, he often accidentally gathers personal information from potential enrollees in the course of gathering basic information to determine eligibility for the program. Often, unintentionally, Richard gleans insights about the suffering in their lives when the folks in the neighborhoods feel that sharing is appropriate or safe for them to do so.

Spending three days a week canvassing these neighborhoods makes Richard nervous. The majority of the neighborhoods that he is assigned to canvass experience the social funneling of gang activity and human trafficking into them. Most people stay indoors to avoid these dangers. He only canvasses during the day and with great attention to his surroundings for both scouting out potential enrollees as well as possible safety issues. When he knocks on doors, he makes families nervous because of these safety issues. His supervisor believes that Richard is safer to be alone in those neighborhoods because of his six-foot, four-inch frame and Afro Latino traits. Richard's not so sure that he agrees with his supervisor's assessment. He wonders if his supervisor knows anything about police violence in these neighborhoods against people who look like him (Gross & Mann, 2017; Sewell, 2017).

There are two ways that Richard's job creates chronic stress and vicarious trauma in his body. That is, first, being in unsafe spaces and, second, learning about the stress and trauma of the people who he is engaging three days a week during canvassing. Firstly, to attempt to keep himself safe, Richard starts the morning by strategizing. He prepares by doing the following:

1. He avoids clothing colors that align with gang territories.
2. He wears a food program hat and lanyard to advertise that he is in the neighborhood for social services reasons.
3. He keeps his personal and work cell phones readily available,

without passcode access required, and in his pockets in case he needs to call for help.

4. He parks his car in strategically located spaces so that he can get back to it quickly, as needed.

This preparatory work is synchronized with Richard's rise in adrenaline before leaving for a day of canvassing. He shares with his girlfriend that even as he is getting ready in the morning to canvass, his body feels like he is getting ready to go into a fight.

To date, Richard sees himself as lucky. The majority of possible safety issues have turned out to be no problem at all. Mostly he experiences benign activities such as when persons panhandling approach him. The solution is easy; he offers a dollar and kind, down-to-Earth words. When random people ask to use his cell phone, he says that he can't lend out his work phone. When he gets a stare from young males in gang affiliated circumstances, he avoids eye contact and moves on quickly. Nonetheless, this regular exposure to unsafe spaces, like the people living in the neighborhoods who he wishes to serve through SNAP enrollment, is a hallmark factor that leads to unmitigated chronic stress and vicarious trauma.

Secondly, standing on sidewalks, crouching down at bus stops, and sitting on porches, Richard learns about the financial and health circumstances of the community members who he is trying to enroll in the food program. He learns about their current income; the last time that they ate a nutritious meal; how often their children eat nutritious meals; the number of people living in their residence; and so forth. Richard must gather this information to compare their circumstances to the program enrollment criteria. From their responses, he sees a basic thumbprint of their daily stress and systemic oppression. Some families also divulge additional information. He estimates about 20 percent of families, depending on the month, also share about their experiences with violence, layoffs, deaths, substance abuse conditions, and mental health issues through the course of answering his questions. He is in spaces where trauma unfolds

---

Chronic Stress and Staying Safe

To attempt to keep himself safe, Richard starts the morning by strategizing; he prepares by doing the following:

1. He avoids clothing colors that align with gang territories.

2. He wears a food program hat and lanyard to advertise that he is in the neighborhood for social services reasons.

3. He keeps his personal and work cell phones readily available, without passcode access required, and in his pockets in case he needs to call for help.

4. He parks his car in strategically located spaces so that he can get back to it quickly, as needed.

and hears and sees it in the lives of the people he engages. They trust Richard enough to share this information because they have seen him many, many times in their neighborhood.

Similar to Tania, Richard's role does not have immediately and clear benchmarks of success aside from meeting a quota level of people approached to possibly enroll in the program. For example, even though Richard takes very serious meeting his daily quota for making contacts and his monthly quota for enrolling families in SNAP, his daily experiences seem like a big failure. He finds it challenging to screen families who face food scarcity but do not necessarily qualify for the program. Unless families meet prescribed benchmarks across income, household size, health, etc., Richard cannot enroll them in the program. In his on-the-ground experience, he sees that many families should be allowed to enroll, but are prevented from doing so by the national food program standards. Further, many families may qualify for the program, but they appear hesitant about sharing private information with Richard, a stranger, so he never can fully engage these families.

Closing

Alex, Tania, Maribel, and Richard share a commitment to serving community members who deserve and need quality nonprofit community-based social services programs in order to navigate oppressive structures that include substantial barriers to health and safety. They also share in the consequences of being committed to fulfilling their job duties in terms of showing up to jobs even with exposure to unmitigated chronic stress and vicarious trauma. Many nonprofit community-based social services professionals who are delivering services and programs experience chronic stress and vicarious trauma like their specialized peers in the healthcare and social work professions that have frequently been the focus of research (Baines et al., 2002).

> *Serving and Suffering*
>
> *It is no surprise that Alex, Tania, Maribel, and Richard are simultaneously loyal to the bigger picture of resolving social inequities through nonprofit community-based social services careers while also suffering from the biological penalties of such.*

It is no surprise, then, that Alex, Tania, Maribel, and Richard are simultaneously loyal to the bigger picture of resolving social inequities through nonprofit community-based social services careers while also suffering from the biological penalties of such. Alex and Tania experience the compounded strain of both expansive workloads as well as the vicarious trauma that comes from partnering closely with traumatized community members. Maribel, some in the nonprofit sector might argue, lucked out the privilege of a 9 a.m. to 5 p.m. workday and mostly remaining in her airconditioned office all day. Unlike her peers in this chapter, she does not travel the city for casework or canvassing, but job role vigilance and exposure to the veteran students' trauma is problematic, nonetheless. Richard finds his workload doable, but his lack of safety and exposure to community members' palpable oppression were not specified in his job description under "canvass."

These four professionals are the real thing. They make the nonprofit sector serve as "forces for good" (Crutchfield & Grant, 2012). Few position descriptions in the social services niche have warning statements about the guarantee of chronic stress and vicarious trauma. Also, the description does not articulate the likelihood of no organizational supports to mitigate the negative impact of that stress and trauma. In fact, although it is ubiquitous, few university nonprofit degree and certification programs even include training on this topic. The cultural beliefs of the nonprofit sector—the deep, deep normalizing of professional suffering while serving—allow the sector to ignore the problem of unmitigated chronic stress and vicarious trauma and avoid doing much about it. National associations and funders within the nonprofit sector are not calling for change. The power of nonprofit cultural beliefs, and the behavioral norms that the beliefs create, becomes a circular investment in keeping the professionals suffering in the name of doing good. These norms ensure that the sector is constantly infusing oppression from the social issues central to the mission of the organizations into the job roles. Where does the sector leadership land on this problem? In future chapters, we continue to explore this. Ultimately, Alex, Tania, Maribel, and Richard—along with the 73 survey respondents—illustrate how the paradox of serving and suffering unfolds in nonprofit community-based social services jobs.

CHAPTER 3

Nonprofit Sector
Cultural Beliefs and Norms

The conversation in this book must also explore how the nonprofit sector cultural beliefs and norms underpin the problem of unmitigated chronic stress and vicarious trauma in nonprofit community-based social services jobs. These sector cultural beliefs and norms carry a fixation on appearing as trying to resolve social ills yet they actually mirror back to us the U.S. historical, industrial fixation on getting the most time and labor from workers. The irony is obvious; the professionals tasked with triaging and transforming social ills are forced to contend with unmitigated chronic stress and vicarious trauma, a sector ill. This chapter supports readers in understanding what cultural beliefs and norms are, how they work in the nonprofit sector, and what we might be able to do about them.

> ### What Is a Cultural Belief?
>
> *A cultural belief is a thought pattern that can be detected among a group through patterned, shared mannerisms and behaviors. The thought pattern is weaved into many mannerisms and behaviors that they are passed to the next generation as seemingly innate and inevitable ways of being.*

It is vital to understand that cultural beliefs and norms in the broader U.S. and western context stem from racism and classism, two central parts of U.S. culture (Dunbar-Ortiz, 2014; DiAngelo, 2019; Shelden & Vélez Young, 2021). Racism and classism are deeply embedded into that fabric of U.S. nonprofit norms because this is how culture works. Culture is comprised of the connections across tangible and

> ### What Is a Norm?
>
> *A norm is an established and prescriptive expectation for group behavior that becomes authoritative through the course of repetition. The use of structures and practices to reify the norms makes the norms appear natural and authoritative.*

intangible materials and symbols that maintain core cultural beliefs for the group. Culture always informs institutions, including medical, legal, and food institutions, even the nonprofit sector. Racism and classism get in the way of mitigating chronic stress and vicarious trauma in terms of the sector's fixation on appearing as if trying to resolve social ills that arise from racism and classism, but again the fixation actually mirrors back to us the U.S. historical, industrial, classist fixation on getting the most time and labor from workers.

Further, executive leadership at the organizational and nonprofit sector levels ensure that the problem remains. That is, when organizational and sector leadership neglect to question and resolve problems such as unmitigated chronic stress and vicarious trauma, then they are in actuality supporting the problem from their power position where action and inaction carries the messages of the sector culture and norms. In the case of unmitigated chronic stress and vicarious trauma, many leaders in the nonprofit social service niche, and major funders of these programs and services, are intentionally forward thinkers, but cannot see the racist and classist practices that they are invested in maintaining (Thornton, 2007; Villanueva, 2017).

The sector cultural beliefs and norms channel attention away from transformative responses to chronic stress and vicarious trauma. Much of the niche has been forced to accept unmitigated chronic stress and vicarious trauma as "natural" and "inevitable" parts to working in nonprofit community-based social services direct service careers. Exploration of the problem requires the deconstruction of nonprofit culture and the norms. A principal norm to explore is *serving and suffering* which is framed among nonprofit community-based social services professionals as not a systemic problem across hundreds of thousands of professionals, but rather as individual problems needing only self-care remedies. Three prominent norms comprise the nonprofit sector and are especially problematic for the social services niche, including the following:

> ### What Is Racism?
>
> *Racism is the practice of organizing people within a human value hierarchy based on perceived biological racial categories, though entirely unscientific, in order to oppress those persons tagged as least valuable in the hierarchy. This hierarchy places whiteness at the top of the hierarchy as the most valued humans. The hierarchy informs structures and practices throughout the society, including all institutions and access to political, economic, and social power.*

- Good people are willing to sacrifice in the course of service.
- Caring for other people is the focus of charitable activities.
- If there was a problem, then leadership would solve it.

These norms are pulled apart for exploration later in this chapter, but fundamentally, the magnitude of the problem requires taking on and resetting cultural beliefs and norms. The first norm, *Good people are willing to sacrifice in the course of service*, is essentially a classist cultural belief, where working laborers into exhaustion is normalized. The second norm, *Caring for other people is the focus of charitable activities*, is at the core a racist cultural belief. This norm focuses the nonprofit organization's response to social inequities, social inequities created from racism, as simply about "caring enough" rather than focusing on adjusting the human value hierarchy and the ways it is used to distribute social, economic, and political power in the community and inside of the organization. The third norm, *If there was a problem, then leadership would solve it*, is also at the core a classist cultural belief. This norm reinforces the power relationship between workers and their managers, where workers hold and/or access less social, economic, and political power to address the tangible needs surrounding unmitigated chronic stress and vicarious trauma.

It is important to explore and deconstruct nonprofit culture and norms so that we can break free from the taken-for-granted-ness of unmitigated chronic stress and vicarious trauma which stems from the same forces that create the social inequities that we are taking on in nonprofit community-based social services work. The three norms listed above originate in Eurocentric industrial production and patriarchal domination of people and resources. The next time that you hear some version of these norms spoken aloud or when you hear the thoughts in your own mind resemble these norms, know that this is the power of creating culture and norms. Culture and norms are supposed to show up in our speech, thought, mannerisms, relationships, and formal and informal rules. This is what culture and norms do for us, for humans. Don't be fooled into positioning these norms as celebrating nonprofit professionals as dedicated to righteous work. These norms are fulfilling the instructions of a racist and classist culture.

Some executive leadership at the organizational and sector levels are attempting to mitigate the negative impact of chronic stress and vicarious trauma and these examples matter. Their examples offer solutions that we all benefit from. Their efforts may be most commendable for the fact that they are pushing against our nonprofit sector's cultural beliefs and norms by democratizing the organization's operations and welcoming non-assimilation to sector norms; for example, within their organizations, some are calling for and incubating innovations that benefit the health and well-being of staff teams. Swimming against the current is something that we all must do to edit the culture and to solve the problem of unmitigated chronic stress and vicarious trauma in nonprofit community-based social services jobs. The examples from these leaders close this chapter.

How Do the Sector Culture and Norms Work?

Researchers have spent lots of time examining the pressures that cultural beliefs and their norms create among groups of people. Conforming to group norms is common even when those norms create difficulties; harms to staff teams are well known. Check out these examples:

- The enforcement of norms can create known physical harm in the job context and yet the norms continue to be reinforced (Hewlin et al., 2016).
- Organizational threats and risks can appear and yet are deprioritized in order to adhere to established organizational norms, all while people and resources are jeopardized (Eller & Frey, 2018).
- Norms inspire staff to give incorrect answers to questions even when the staff persons know the correct responses (Tsunogaya et al., 2017).

Ironies exist within any group's culture and norms, allowing all of us to hold even greater appreciation for the leadership models of some in the nonprofit sector that are discussed at the end of this chapter. As will be fleshed out further in this chapter, by consciously countering the cultural beliefs of racism and classism and the resulting norms, everyone in the sector gets permission to go against, or say something contrary about, nonprofit norms surrounding unmitigated chronic stress and vicarious trauma. The nonprofit sector norms that create barriers to resolving chronic stress and vicarious trauma are embraced by the majority of us

> ### Can You Find Nonprofit Community-Based Social Services Norms?
>
> *Go looking for subtle interactions, activities, and rhetoric about*
>
> - *grinding through your day;*
> - *low pay for a job that's supposedly about "caring" for poor and BIPOC communities; and*
> - *waiting for your leadership to help you.*

who comprise the sector, even when the norms are counter to our own well-being, go against science, and distract us from practical solutions.

The nonprofit sector culture and norms are deeply embedded in our interactions through conversations, job descriptions, interpersonal relationships, organizational policies or lack of policies, etc. Go looking for obvious and subtle aspects of racism and classism in your professional experience of unmitigated chronic stress and vicarious trauma. They are weaved into the ordinariness of our daily schedules. That's why we, as a sector, so successfully allow chronic stress and vicarious trauma to go largely unaddressed among the precious change makers who comprise the workforce of social services professionals. This conversation of the culture and norms also matters because the solutions presented in later chapters must be wielded thoughtfully in order to contend with the powerful influence of culture and norms. Editing culture is no simple task.

Norms create a sense of what is normal for everyday job interactions. As professionals, we learn to speak, hear, and enact the established culture and norms. The patterned thoughts that serve as instructions for speaking, hearing, and acting, allow us to know what expectations exist for each actor in the theater piece. Like a well-rehearsed play, the actors, or the professionals, can predict what happens before and after common, daily interactions and activities. For example, many social services professionals would report that they do not speak ill of their organization's executive leadership's lack of support because the professionals themselves would be socially shamed for condemning a hard at work nonprofit. Another example includes that many social services professionals know that to express that they are "stressed" and "overworked" is just fine, but any further analysis of the situation would be bizarre because to be "stressed" and "overworked" is normalized.

> *Norms Can Prevent Questions*
>
> *We collectively ensure a uniform melody is played by aligning nonprofit structures and practices with the mythology and norms. This melody keeps the unmitigated chronic stress and vicarious trauma largely unquestioned.*

Norms and Collective Tuning Forks

Our normalized, expected speaking, hearing, and acting in the workplace tunes us, as individuals and as a collective, to the harmony of the nonprofit sector culture. Like tuning forks, our speaking, hearing, and acting is informed by the widespread adoption of the culture and norms all around us and then reinforce the assumed validity of the norms. Round and round we go. This is not human insanity. Instead, this is how groups maintain shared understandings, values, and predict group cohesion. In the nonprofit sector and in all large groups, we collectively ensure a uniform melody is played by aligning nonprofit structures and practices with the nonprofit culture and norms through patterned speaking, hearing, and acting. You and me, we play our role in the theater piece, and we do it well.

We are collective tuning forks through our speech, what we listen for, and our chosen behavior; we are all culpable. The melody that we co-create keeps the unmitigated chronic stress and vicarious trauma largely unquestioned. Reviewing how norms work helps us to understand the resistance that we may face when challenging sector norms with the very colleagues that we care so much about.

How culture and norms work is very straightforward: Norms norm us. Norms are one of the most magical things that we create as human beings. The need for socializing, to exist predictably within groups, requires norms. Norms in and of themselves are not the threat. Rather, the instructions that are housed within norms are vital to understand. These instructions inform the members of the group which speech, interactions, and behaviors are acceptable and which are not. The instructions can also provide reminders of the rewards and punishments for abiding by the norms. And sometimes, the instructions seem contradictory; recall the three examples from above where norms can drive anyone to go against their own and their group's best interests in the workplace context.

Think about norms in a common context such as within the family. For example, all families have norms, whatever the size of the family. Without ever being explicitly told "here are the norms for our family," we know how to walk into a room, when to quip back in sarcasm and when not to, which sounds alert us to risk or safety, and so forth. Parents who are reading this book have watched their children mirror back these norms without ever providing a PowerPoint presentation on the how and when to perform the family norms. Though, on occasion, parents might hear themselves say, "In this family, we don't [fill in the blank]." Through our patterned speech, the cues we listen for, and our behavior, we attune

> ### Norms Are Sneaky
>
> *Norms can be formally presented through structures such as policies and tools. However, norms are frequently presented informally through behavior like conversations and nuances within interpersonal exchanges.*

ourselves to the family norms. And, and, and, when we do *not* attune ourselves, our choices are noticed.

More examples from within the workplace show the ways that we frequently serve as a collective of tuning forks. Sometimes the most powerful of norms come into focus through observation when we are new to the group. First, we don't need anyone to tell us the group's culture or receive a presentation about the organizational culture. We can find the culture and its norms on our own. Some norms are formally communicated through organizational policies, practices, and even documents such as job descriptions. There can be literal, official documents that state in some way, "Here's how we [fill in the blank]." For example, here are norms made very clear in formal documentation:

- a dress code policy;
- the hours of operation;
- workflow expectations; and
- prescribed project management deliverables.

The content inside each of the four examples shows a range of norms, including norms about visual appearance, when staff should be at their desks looking busy, the team's logic around ordering different aspects of a project, and the focus of projects and use of project funds.

When we are new to an organization, or new to a level of responsibility within an organization, we can pick up on the trickiest of norms, the informal ones. Informal norms tell us, like with the example above with a family unit, how to walk into a conference room, when to make one's self sound strategic versus tactical, which word choices alert us to risk or safety, and so forth. As we will see from three colleagues—Chelsea, Felipe, and Elliott—professionals do not often communicate formally, or directly, on the nonprofit sector culture of racism and classism and the three norms outlined at the outset:

- Good people are willing to sacrifice in the course of service.
- Caring for other people is the focus of charitable activities.
- If there was a problem, then leadership would solve it.

The norms are not directly spoken. Listening to their conversation, however, we can hear our colleagues relay the norms like whispers that make a subtle presence in a space. In the short examples below, the exhaustion, fatigue, and literal physical hunger from Chelsea, Felipe, and Elliott is presented in their speech as commonplace, inevitable, and "natural." Yet, even with the perceived "naturalness" of norms, we can deconstruct spoken words and patterned behavior in order to understand which of the norms are being lived out in their workspace.

For example, how could Felipe do his job successfully if he was not straining every one of his physical and mental capacities to resolve emergency situations with clients? Readers can see in the example of these three colleagues the ways that nonprofit sector norms can be expressed through speech and interactions even when the norm does not serve the people expressing the speech. In particular, we can see in this example that the professionals' work activities were equating job-based suffering with effective job performance. This norm is well embraced in nonprofit sector culture.

Informal Norms Have the Trickiest Patterns to Notice

At the end of a long day, around a long conference table, and on the tail-end of the professionals resolving serious challenges faced by their clients, Chelsea, Felipe, and Elliott illustrate an informal means for enforcing norms. They sit around the conference table where Chelsea eventually reaches for the cookies at the center of the table, "See, Felipe, it's your fault. I'm trying, but you bring these."

Felipe is known as the snack provider, knowing very well that snacks keep tired colleagues engaged and that true mealtimes are rare at the rate in which he and his colleagues move. "Did you eat lunch?" he responds with a chiding tone. Though she hears him, Chelsea doesn't respond verbally nor looks up from her laptop. "See?" Felipe offers.

Chelsea's attempts at avoiding snacks that do not align with her dieting efforts are well-known among the team. But also well known, displayed by Felipe's response, is that few of them take time to eat meals.

"After this morning, I deserve the whole friggin' box," Elliott offers. The group laughs at his quip. They are all aware of the emergency response he was involved with earlier this afternoon with several youth clients; the morning events were an important and significant show of his skills, but exhausting and dreaded by all of the professionals at the table.

Felipe rounds out the conversation as he chews a cookie, "That's how it goes," framing the eating of the cookies as the only salve for the "natural" workplace suffering, its constant, uninterrupted presence in their work lives.

Hundreds of thousands of nonprofit community-based social services professionals invoke this norm, and as humorously as Chelsea, Felipe, and Elliott. Humor is also a constant in their work lives. While in earlier chapters readers saw the ways that nonprofit sector norms show up in structures such as job requirements and in implementing those require- ments, with the three colleagues we see the norm play out in speech and behavior. The professionals invoked the norm of *serving and suffering* as "natural." With disheveled hair and clothing, sitting around the con- ference table, the awareness that many in the room had not eaten their lunches or used the restroom in hours highlights the link between the banter on cookies and client emergencies with nonprofit norms. The daily suffering is so common that the professionals mostly accept the pain and focus back on the people who they are serving.

Norms Communicate the Culture

Norms are sneaky in that they go largely undetected to most of us unless we violate them. This is the magic of norms; they norm our lives without us realizing that we are collectively agreeing to carry the mel- ody that becomes prescriptive. For decades, researchers have explored the ways that groups such as families, sport teams, and employees co-create their norms. Most often, we inherit the norms of the group members who came before us. Consider again the family example; for generations a fam- ily can engage in norms that are historical only because no previous gen- eration decided to edit those norms. The phrasing "We've always done it this way" might show up in family gatherings pertaining to how enchila- das are cooked, the ways children are taught to swim, and the acceptability or lack thereof of LGBTQ+ family members living an open and affirming life within the family.

During the last decade, more attention has been paid by research- ers to the ways that a group's norms impact the group's health and well-being (Haslam, 2014). For better or for worse, nonprofit teams can be aided by norms that advance health or oppressed by them. When col- leagues see themselves as "normal," they are less likely to question the existence and function of the norms that they are performing moment by moment. Further, members of a group are likely to be less willing to let go of those norms when offered new struc- tures, practices, or behaviors that

> ___The Power of Group Norms___
>
> *Even if there is a safety or legal issue faced by an organization, and should act as a motivation to edit the culture, the threat of dan- ger or legal liability is often not persuasive enough to overcome the human commitment to group norms (Choi et al., 2017).*

better serve them as individuals or collectively as a team. Creating new norms requires a lot because this is the editing of the culture. Cultural beliefs as strong as racism and classism have norms dedicated to upholding the culture. Changing norms is not just about taking on new structures, practices, or behaviors. Most painfully for groups, changing norms means admitting that the cultural beliefs and norms exist, that they do not serve the group or the group's new desire, and that a new, even unknown cultural belief will be adopted. Even if there is a safety or legal issue faced by an organization, and should act as a motivation to edit the culture, the threat of danger or legal liability is often not persuasive enough to overcome the human commitment to group norms (Choi et al., 2017).

Commitment to group norms is what makes norms reliable containers for groups, and those who come after them, to live in. Thanks again to the curiosities of researchers, the interpersonal and socializing dynamics that we engage in as human beings has been studied and found to be linked to our health outcomes (i.e., "social determinants of health") (Marmot, 2015). Understanding that our group norms are linked to our health outcomes allows us to experiment with rearranging, rewriting, and reimagining norms in order to meaningfully solve health and well-being issues at the group, and hopefully, societal levels.

No matter how skilled—and nonprofit professionals are highly skilled, hold immense amounts of wisdom, sometimes carry degrees and certifications, and work relentlessly to serve people in the community—these professionals are vulnerable to the nonprofit culture and norms just as all human beings are. In fact, we are all primed to support the attunement of our group's culture and norms. Our work-related suffering from unmitigated chronic stress and vicarious trauma is "natural" and "inevitable" *only* within the boundaries of our sector's cultural beliefs.

The Three Norms Carried Inside of Nonprofit Sector Culture

The mission of this book is to point out the mythology and norms, the expected or "natural" part of the nonprofit community-based social services job. The nonprofit mythology naturalizes and makes inevitable the suffering of the professionals. Yet, serving and suffering *is not* required. Cue Chelsea, Felipe, and Elliott to eat cookies for momentary reprieve. The sacrifice of their health and well-being is anchored to our sector historically. The historical lineage which underpins the problem of unmitigated chronic stress and vicarious trauma among nonprofit community-based social services professionals is detectable through pulling apart the three norms.

Norm 1: Good people are willing to sacrifice in the course of service.

Unmitigated chronic stress and vicarious trauma is visible through observation and reported in anonymous surveys. The norm that serving people through one's calling requires suffering unfortunately waves away concern for the professionals and the sustainability of their work. Let's look deeper. What is the U.S. history with racism and classism that feeds the norm of *suffering while serving*?

Christianizing settlers were part of a larger white population of colonizers who brought this norm with them as part of the force that put in motion nearly 400 years of historical trauma in North America. In the official framing of this norm, the norm was that the Christianizing settlers were willing to serve a divine calling no matter the cost to their own comfort with establishing their religion. Dr. Dunbar-Ortiz, in her book *An Indigenous People's History of the United States* (2014), provides a careful documentation of what this norm looked like for the Christianizing colonizers, their non-evangelical counterparts, and the colonized societies across time and geography. Importantly, the official Puritan norms profoundly set into motion traumatizing for generations and laid the foundation for which the U.S. was eventually established. The official norming is clear through the

> ### Self-Sacrifice
>
> *Self-sacrifice at a job that is supposedly about "caring" for people must contend with the history of this norm which stems from the brutality against BIPOC communities. In the U.S. cultural context, self-sacrificing cannot be separated from the historical norms that inform the institutions born through U.S. cultural commitment to racism and classism.*

wealth of historical documentation that Dr. Dunbar-Ortiz provides; anyone who was not part of the established group, with this prescribed white Christian paradigm, violated group norms and was offered up for violence and genocide.

Researchers who focus on the consequences of religious oppression illustrate the long-term pain that is created. The "good people" prescription within the norm is dangerous for the ways it involves both a moralistic self-sacrificing but also weaves in a history of destruction for Black, indigenous, and persons of color (BIPOC) in the U.S. society. That is, this norm in this U.S. cultural context is used in the nonprofit community-based social services niche to enforce self-sacrificing even though it is rooted in the U.S. cultural priority with damaging the existence of original civilizations in North America (Harvey & Rivett, 2017).

Further, this norm is powerful for its paternalism embedded in the notion of serving under divine instruction, paternalism over indigenous civilizations and Black bodies. We must recognize the link between this norm framed as self-sacrificing in the course of service *and* the brutality of forcing entire civilizations to sacrifice their origins for the implementation of white supremacy in North America. "Service" in the historical context of white Christianizing colonizers equates with genocide. Self-sacrifice and brutality go together in U.S. culture because of the historical context in which this norm was born. Self-sacrifice at a job that is supposedly about "caring" for people must contend with the history of this norm which stems from the brutality against BIPOC communities. In the U.S. cultural context, self-sacrificing cannot be separated from the historical norms that inform the institutions born through the U.S. cultural commitment to racism and classism. That is, the European industrial revolution and colonization model overworks vulnerable populations, in the past and presently. This model, obviously, also denies support like the failure to mitigate chronic stress and vicarious trauma. The white supremacy focus within a nonprofit community-based social services organization assumes that it is natural and inevitable for organizational teams to exhibit efficiency, individualism, fear of conflict, defensiveness, and urgency (Okum, n.d.). The white supremacy values are not able to support your organizational mission that, in some way, centers on transforming social inequities such as racism and classism.

Chelsea, Felipe, and Elliott illustrate the pervasiveness of Norm 1. The norm is foundational in the U.S. nonprofit community-based social services niche. The cookie eating example serves as a subtle placeholder for many, many related scenarios where some version of Felipe's "That's how it goes" is stated. "That's how it goes" reflects and reinforces the instruction that *serving and suffering* go together. The tension, fatigue, need for soothing through simple carbs, and missed meals and restroom breaks are taken as evidence of being a good person (i.e., suffering) and an effective professional (i.e., serving). Hence, the lack of structures, practices, and behaviors to mitigate chronic stress and vicarious trauma in nonprofit community-based social services jobs makes sense. According to Norm 1, these professionals are supposed to suffer in order to indicate, in alignment with U.S. culture, that important community work is happening and is happening upon populations who require colonizing.

Because the history and culture that created this norm exercised brutality, we can pull on earlier discussions in this book in terms of nonprofit community-based social services professionals focusing their talents on triaging and transforming social inequities. The oppression of populations by class, race, gender bias, and so forth is what makes nonprofit community-based social services organizations so badly needed in the U.S. Even though the link to brutality within Norm 1 is not intended by Chelsea, Felipe, and Elliott, they enact the culture through the norm.

Norm 2: Caring for other people is the focus of charitable activities.

The second norm in nonprofit sector culture has a cumulative effect on nonprofit community-based social services professionals where self-sacrificing as well as "caring" for the well-being of community members become entangled and exhausting for the professionals. Ultimately, "caring" is about classism in that the caring professions such as teaching, hospice, case management, social work, and child care have some of the lowest paid jobs in this country. Tagging nonprofit community-based social services professionals as part of the caring professions assigns these professionals less economic power along with teachers, social workers, etc.

At the outset of this book, chronic stress and vicarious trauma is estimated to be here to stay. That is, in order to authentically partner with people in the direct delivery of a service or program, the professionals must move into close proximity of the stress and trauma experienced by the people. Hence, perhaps "caring" about people is in fact a major focus of nonprofit community-based social services professionals, yet tagging the professionals as "caring" rather than something like "strategically transforming social inequities" resonates too closely with diminishing the power held by these professionals across class standing in the U.S. Tagging the professionals as "caring" aligns with the U.S. cultural context of classism and racism—apparently jobs that transform social inequities experienced by people living in poverty and disproportionately by BIPOC brothers and sisters are not jobs worthy of economic power.

Further, "caring" for people through early U.S. charity outlets, a precursor to the nonprofit sector, started with churches and then religiously adjacent institutions such as colleges and hospitals. Peoples who were the focus of charity work in the 17th and 18th centuries were populations already stigmatized such as people living in poverty, immigrants, and sometimes those who were disabled (Nodoushani et al., 2019). A review of the U.S. historical context for the birthing of Norm 2 allows us to consider the invention of the word "charity" which focused attention at the "unlucky" people who lived in poverty. This oversimplification is with us today and shows an ahistorical and apolitical invention of the U.S. use of the word *charity*. Even though charity has been used as a word and concept since about the 12th century in Western Europe, the use in the North American context pre- and post-the founding of the U.S. made "caring" for "charitable" purposes more about essentializing already oppressed persons as inferior and in need of colonizing services.

In order to deconstruct Norm 2, comprised of classist and racist cultural beliefs, it is important to consider unmitigated chronic stress and vicarious trauma among nonprofit community-based social services professionals. Consider first that "caring" about community members does not have to be coupled to unmitigated suffering for the professionals. Perhaps the suffering that comes through vicarious trauma is a guarantee in these job roles, but this does not need to be unmitigated. Second, all social services professionals are part of a collective effort to address social inequities, whether or not that is in the organizational mission statement or in job descriptions. We must flip the "caring" for people norm; we must no longer allow ourselves to be forced to reiterate and perform this norm. Instead, nonprofit community-based social services professionals "partner" with systematically oppressed persons and their job support must include facilitating resources to ensure the sustainability of the professionals doing this important "partnering" work. Cautiously, we must understand that the influence of nonprofit culture and norms hide the classism and racism central to nonprofit operations, making "caring" appear legitimate; it is up to us to open a window into this Norm 2, peek inside, and see the historical oppressions choreographing much of nonprofit culture.

Unmitigated chronic stress and vicarious trauma is so well supported by Norm 1 and Norm 2. That is, the fallout for the professionals is refashioned to reinforce self-sacrifice and "caring" are noble acts. However, these norms serve the colonial project by making the seemingly noble acts look like a reflection of righteous suffering integral to the purpose of the nonprofit sector. We already know that the frequency of chronic stress and vicarious trauma among nonprofit social service professionals in direct service jobs is significant. We also already know that nonprofit organizations rarely challenge this norm. We saw this in the work lives of Alex, Tania, Maribel, and Richard. Many readers also see this in their current nonprofit organizations; the silent acceptance of *serving and suffering* can change when we point to the cultural beliefs and norms underpinning the problem.

Norm 3: If there was a problem, then the leaders would solve it.

Hierarchy and a highly structured chain of command are also the heritage of colonizers. The punitive theme of early colonizers, their policies, and practices informed the birthing of the U.S. through cultural instructions that impact many sectors of society, beyond religious establishments and nonprofits (Putney, 2009). Importantly, Norms 1 through 3, that drive the nonprofit sector, do so through a shared historical channel. That is, the colonizers of North America and their belief systems created a hegemony that

> #### What Is "Hegemony"?
>
> *"Hegemony" is a structured system where a small group becomes dominant over the larger population in terms of cultural imagery, political resources, economic strength, etc. The larger population, the mass, does not resist in any major way because the structured system prevents such with benefits and threats (Gramsci, 2010).*
>
> *"[W]e understand hegemony as those in power who are free to establish their master narrative, which dictates not only who belongs to a society but also who does not" (Shear et al., 2015).*

we operate our nonprofit community-based organizations within today.

Let's think through Norm 3 in terms of the U.S. historical basis. To defer decision-making to authority figures is the hallmark of a hegemonic society where the mass reinforces the power-holder's control, adhering to the expectations set up by the power-holders through all layers of the society including economics, politics, culture, medicine, etc. (Cobas et al., 2009; Gramsci, 2010; Shear et al., 2015). When staff teams define "leadership" as a small group of people who are assigned to make the best decisions, decisions that are supposed to be for the best interest of the organizational mission, it turns out that staff teams recuse themselves from informing their organization's solutions. Solutions often come from those with the closest proximity to problems like nonprofit community-based social services professionals in direct service roles rather than those with executive job titles. Even those with executive job titles who once served in direct service roles often drink the hegemony Kool-Aid in order to fit the nonprofit sector culture.

The unmitigated chronic stress and vicarious trauma among these professionals is allowed by leaderships' buy-in of nonprofit culture. Here is a clear voice on the dangers of Norm 3 if our goal is to dismantle oppression: "consolidation of responsibility and power in the people who occupy those [top leadership] positions [creates a definition of leadership as] focus on administration.... This myopic view of leadership also makes it hard to see the leadership qualities exhibited on a daily basis by people in all positions within our organizations" (Mont, 2017). The myopic approach to leadership activities is normalized by offloading problems (i.e., unmitigated chronic stress and vicarious trauma) and their possible solutions to organizational leaders.

Funders and donors, directly and indirectly, are the main audience for most nonprofit executive leadership. This is the audience that receives the most attention in nonprofit community-based social services organizations. Expecting executive leadership to actually understand what it is like for direct service professionals to effectively serve community members, on the ground, is unreasonable. The executive leadership create structures and practices, and encourage behavior, that serve their audience's desires rather than inquire into what approaches are needed for the longer view of social change (Villanueva, 2018). Questioning the beliefs and behaviors of the chain of command in many nonprofits will not likely be celebrated. Punishment for violating the hegemony, like the heritage of Norm 3 shows us, is the possible consequence for questioning the chain of command. Executive leaders, whether or not consciously, are expected to carry out the speech and behaviors of proper power-holders.

Community members are the main audience for nonprofit social services. The professionals are frequently fully consumed by partnering with community members, so much so that they are distracted from actively addressing or advocating for resolving the nonprofit sector norms and the adjoining unmitigated chronic stress and vicarious trauma, no matter how contrary the norms are to transforming social inequities.

Discussion of Norm 3 can also shine light on the pressures that often restrict leaders from engaging in substantive changes to improve the nonprofit sector culture. These pressures on top of organizational leadership are chronicled in two

> *Professionals Aren't Duped*
>
> *Chelsea, Felipe, and Elliott are not duped into the norms; rather, they are transporters of a highly attuned melody that flows throughout the nonprofit sector.*

21st century books that illustrate the powerful backing of Norm 3, *The Revolution Will Not Be Funded: Beyond the Non-Profit Industrial Complex* (Thornton, 2007) and *Decolonizing Wealth: Indigenous Wisdom to Heal Divides and Restore Balance* (Villanueva, 2021). These important books illustrate the ways that externally birthed political and financial forces function inside the nonprofit sector. These forces, as the books carefully outline, directly influence nonprofit sector norms because leaders model and reinforce the norms, especially Norm 3, as legitimate, "natural," and inevitable.

Nonprofit cultural beliefs, norms, and their historical origins are allowed to live in our daily lives through structures, practices, and behaviors. Chelsea, Felipe, and Elliott are not duped into the norms; rather, they are transporters of a highly attuned melody that flows throughout the nonprofit sector. They are not ignorant to other professional options that exist for them where unmitigated chronic stress and vicarious trauma are less likely. They are, however, committed to upholding the norms of nonprofit sectors because that is how hegemony works; that is, the mass, like Chelsea, Felipe, and Elliott, do not resist the power structure because of perceived benefits and threats to job security.

Leadership Models That Counter the Nonprofit Sector Culture and Norms

While exploring nonprofit sector culture and norms, which deliver on the instructions of a racist and classist lineage, it is important to also study those who are shepherding alternative ways to facilitate partnerships with historically oppressed communities. Those who are shaking up the assumption that *unmitigated* chronic stress and vicarious trauma are invaluable role models for the entire nonprofit sector. Understanding who they are, what they are doing, and what we can learn from them can fuel creativity. When reading through the two examples below, never underestimate the influence of the culture and its norms because, most often, culture wins every time as the masses typically reinforce the cultural belief system.

Example 1: Unionizing nonprofit professionals.

The problem of unmitigated chronic stress and vicarious trauma among nonprofit community-based social services professionals is not a problem of self-care or self-help. Let me repeat: The problem of unmitigated chronic stress and vicarious trauma among nonprofit community-based social services professionals is never going to be solved at the individual self-care level. In this first example, we get to learn about an organization, its internal workings, and its work to empower more organizations to unionize. The president of Nonprofit Professional Employees Union (NPEU), Kayla Blado, emphasizes that the Union's mission is not to solve the systemic health crises among non-profit professionals with an individualistic lens; this problem is not an individual's lack of caring for themselves. We know this because health crises for employee and work-based stress is a widespread problem across the U.S., a widespread problem that is embedded into position descriptions and workflows in nonprofit jobs.

Real solutions to this problem require altering structures, practices, and behaviors. Non-solutions to this problem are those things that promote personal responsibility such as taking enough walks at the end of the day. The NPEU warns against self-care notions that oversimplify the problem and solutions because oversimplifying prologues the employee health problems. The union model for nonprofits promotes "com[ing] together with your fellow workers and colleagues and negotiat[ing] organization-wide agreements that help everyone" (Meiksins, 2019). An important question asked, and perhaps answered, is "Do [nonprofit executive leaders] perhaps feel guilty for exploiting workers while supposedly working to improve a community's quality?" (Meiksins, 2019). This is an important question to answer. Precursors to nonprofit unionizing have existed for some time in the form of nonprofit cooperatives. These alternatives to the mainstream nonprofit organizational design allow the professionals to decide democratically what is and is not urgent, what measurable production is and is not valuable, and so forth. The possibilities for nonprofit professionals can significantly alter the nonprofit sector culture and norms.

The three nonprofit norms—Good people are willing to sacrifice in the course of service; caring for other people is the focus of charitable activities; if there was a problem, then leadership would solve it—cannot easily exist in policies, speech, actions, and relationships in a unionized space. Self-sacrifice, a singular focus on caring, and unquestioned power-holding can be explicitly analyzed by an organizational team when a value is placed on uprooting any and all policies and practices that exploit professionals while supposedly working in service to communities.

Example 2: Rising Again Center.

Unmitigated chronic stress and vicarious trauma within nonprofit community-based organizations is not a problem outside of solutions. Solutions exist and we find them when we step beyond the take-for-granted-ness of the nonprofit sector culture and norms. Rising Again Center (RAC), a northern California non-profit community-based organization enacts their organizational mission both externally through their pro-gramming and internally through their employee policies and practices. For example, their mission is to "impact educational attainment and health benchmarks for neighborhood youth while advocating to decrease risk factors" and their three programs are designed to fulfill the mission. Also, the six practices listed below illus-trate the ways that their mission is turned inward, creating a coherent mis-sion presence among the professionals delivering the programming. Specifically, readers get to see that "impact[ing] educational attainment and health benchmarks" is reflected in the six practices.

> ### Engage Professionals as Whole Humans
>
> *Organizational heroes, like NPEU and RAC, illustrate what it looks like to craft and cultivate opportunities that are alternatives to nonprofit sector norms. These two examples show how to engage people as whole humans rather than only workers for the fulfill-ment of racist and classist culture.*

The following six practices are means for mitigating chronic stress and vicarious trauma. The RAC team's shared wisdom is demonstrated through their collective modeling of wellness even in the midst of some of the hardest professional roles, that of altering children's lives and tra-jectories in the neighborhood and temporary housing context that are rife with human and drug trafficking. Throughout the week with members of the RAC team, we can see many policies and practices that defy Norms 1 through 3, including these:

- view trauma research documentaries with facilitated post-viewing discussions;
- participate in Tension and Trauma Release Exercises (TRE) classes with an external trainer;
- participate in spiritual healing workshops with an external facilitator;
- engage in recreational activities that benefit each professional's well-being, activities determined on an individual level half a day per week;

- participate in walking meetings for one-on-one supervision and coaching sessions, every other week; and
- sit quietly in the on-site garden.

Do paychecks get signed? Yes. Do grant funds and outcomes reporting get processed? Yes. However, can you, the reader, imagine walking through your daily professional activities that also include the six organizational practices listed above? The founder and executive director shared that he has been told by many nonprofit executives elsewhere in the sector, on multiple occasions, that he does things "backwards," including the priorities involved in building the administrative infrastructure, partnering with the neighborhood, and supporting the staff team. Investing in the RAC staff team equates to investing in the organizational mission. That is, RAC promotes that "staff health is part of the organizational strategy."

There is so much more RAC can teach us about the embodiment of their belief system and norms. All of our teams could learn from their alternative to the nonprofit sector culture. Ultimately, RAC makes countering Norms 1 through 3 observable through their policies and practices; their alternative approaches are palpable in the ways that the professionals are engaged as whole human beings. Every member of their team is invited to speak, fully experience their positionality in the group, and accept the wisdom of the positionality of those around them. This is why RAC is a strong example to include alongside of the NPEU; both propose leadership models that all nonprofit community-based social services organizations can learn from.

Closing

The heroes in this discussion are foremost the nonprofit community-based social services professionals who are working in the paradox of a situation where they acclimated to norms that hurt them and their long-term contributions to oppressed communities. Nodding at that reality of unmitigated chronic stress and vicarious trauma while snacking on cookies reflects their practicality, commitment, and conundrum. It is really those who set organizational priorities who can make powerful shifts in community-based workplaces. Later in this book, solutions through the use of tools are presented for the individual level, like for the Chelseas, Felipes, and Elliotts of our sector, as well as for leaders at the organizational and sector leadership.

Organizational heroes, like NPEU and RAC, illustrate what it looks like to craft and cultivate opportunities that are alternatives to nonprofit sector norms. These two examples show how to engage people as whole humans rather than only workers for the fulfillment of racist and classist culture. These two examples also show how to prioritize health and well-being for the precious professionals carrying out organizational missions. The nonprofit sector norms that make chronic stress and vicarious trauma expected, and force professionals to accepted unmitigated exposure to them, require attention by all of us, all persons throughout all layers of the nonprofit sector. Altering these norms also significantly lies with the voices of Boards of Directors, funders, and professional associations. These voices go far and carry officialdom needed to edit rhetoric which has claimed the story of American "charitable" work.

> **Professionals Acclimate to Nonprofit Sector Norms**
>
> *The heroes in this discussion are foremost the nonprofit community-based social services professionals who are working in the paradox of a situation where they acclimated to norms that hurt them and their long-term contributions to oppressed communities.*

Nonprofit leaders, at the organizational and sector levels, are the power holders in many ways because they inform the priorities of Boards of Directors, funders, and professional associations and frequently reinforce racist and classist cultural norms. As leaders in these positions of authority, their voices reach further than those of Chelsea, Felipe, and Elliott, as do their paychecks and the symbolic meaning that their paychecks afford. These leaders access audiences that touch the work lives of nonprofit professionals through ordinary means discussed in this book (i.e., job descriptions, grant deliverables, employment policies, etc.). Informing and reinforcing racist and classist cultural norms perpetuates the need for a workforce that is forced into addressing generationally unchanged social inequities decade after decade and, hence, exposing nonprofit community-based social services professionals to job roles framed around chronic stress and vicarious trauma. This perpetuation from leaders in Boards of Directors, funders, and professional associations roles make unmitigated chronic stress and vicarious trauma appear "normal" and "natural."

Returning to the leaders at the organizational level, NPEU and RAC would point out that most executive directors are skilled in explaining overhead costs and the relevancy of these costs for resolving oppressions that their organizations are focused on. Resolving oppressions costs something for office space and technology, paychecks for the professionals, travel and materials to operate programs, and data specialists and marketing geniuses. Responding to the requests for reducing overhead is on the minds of many organizational leaders who must answer to funders, current and potential. This often forces attention and willingness to invest away from healthy and supported staff teams to, instead, providing only the bare minimum of support which equates to unmitigated chronic stress and vicarious trauma.

CHAPTER 4

Tools for Individuals

By this point in the book, many readers want to know what they can individually do to mitigate the fallout from chronic stress and vicarious trauma stemming from their current nonprofit community-based social services careers. This chapter serves those readers, focusing on 17 science-backed tools that can be engaged across distinct settings, lifestyles, and diverse personalities with attention to how to apply each tool and the financial cost of each. Further, for many readers from indigenous heritages, many of these tools don't require the science backing because the tools are already part of our lives. Where this is the case, discussions on the indigenous roots are presented in a very abbreviated manner; my ancestors say that it is just fine to offer abbreviated information for the sake of sharing these tools widely in this book's format.

Warning: If I hear the phrase "personal responsibility" one more time as the solution to unmitigated chronic stress and vicarious trauma, I might lose my mind. This chapter should not be implemented without a clear understanding of the organizational and sector wide responsibilities that go hand in hand with an individual's approach to addressing chronic stress and vicarious trauma stemming from their nonprofit community-based social services work. The power to address your health and well-being resides in your hands as well as in your organization's culture and resource priorities *and* the push-and-pull racist and classist agendas that create the need for nonprofit labor. When an organization formally or informally required Jesse to canvas in unsafe neighborhoods without proper support, Jesse doesn't have the formal discretionary power to educate his employer and/or change his job description and/or change organizational policies and procedures around canvassing. Hence, this chapter should not be read as positioning the solutions to unmitigated chronic stress and vicarious trauma as an

> *"Personal Responsibility"*
> This chapter should not be read as positioning the solutions to unmitigated chronic stress and vicarious trauma as an individual's responsibility.

individual's responsibility. This chapter is dedicated to you and your great capacity to contribute to sustained social transformation, but you are not to blame for the state of your well-being. Remember that medical and social sciences show us that your health and well-being are complex as is the social change work that you do each day.

Further, this chapter is not suggesting that compliance, follow through, or the actual implementation of the tools is easy-peasy. This chapter is designed to make the curated tools straightforward to understand and easy to return to as a reference book for years to come. Research shows that, frequently, our noncompliance in terms of not implementing tools and/or protocols can be up to 70 percent (Holtzman et al., 2015; Martin et al., 2005). That's a 30 percent success rate with implementing tools in our lives! Even when we individually or collectively agree that a tool and/or protocol is important for us as individuals or groups, like hand washing in hospitals as seemingly ironically as that sounds, noncompliance is higher than we would likely hope (i.e., ranging 34 percent to 75 percent with handwashing) (McGuckin et al., 2009; McLaws et al., 2018). Short- and long-term compliance is tricky. The daily demands from our routines, surprises, and emergencies can easily restrict the most disciplined among us.

As readers engage the two sections of tools in this chapter, keep in mind that surrounding one's self with as many science-backed tools as possible will be of tremendous support; surrounding ourselves with these 17 tools helps us to test out tools until some of them stick. Those that stick will fit the unique aspects of each of our circumstances, personalities, and job passions.

Tool Curation Methods

The tools in this chapter were curated for nonprofit professionals in social services job roles with several things in mind. First, nearly all of these tools will be new to readers and attempt to avoid wellness graveyards of pleasant ideas and expensive options. The health and wellness rhetoric in this country has been dominated by elites and their recreational pastimes, coated with strategies that are faddish and without lasting results. Second, most of the tools in this chapter are free, acknowledging that the common nonprofit community-based social services paycheck doesn't leave much room for extras. Third, the tools are reflected in research studies that can inspire confidence in our use of them; nonprofit folks love data and facts for guiding us to what makes a sustainable change in our community-focused work so let's rely on research studies in this same way, for sustainable change options. Fourth, many of the tools curated here are also culturally backed; readers will notice the gifts of many of our cultural heritages have provided to us for sustained well-being. Fifth, the tools can be used collectively with colleagues, friends, and even our furry friends. Many of us come from collective cultures where group time matters; we don't have to engage in wellness trends that promote individualism unless that really fits our lifestyle and needs.

The chapter is split into two sets of tools: *On the Go* and *A Bit More Time.* As the section titles suggest, some of the science-based tools are incredibly practical and can be woven into a day while speeding along your routines. The second set of tools in this

> ### *Science and Culture*
> *Many of the tools curated here are also culturally backed; readers will notice the gifts of many of our cultural heritages, provided to us for sustained well-being.*

chapter requires designated time and planning, but are still practical for nonprofit professionals and our busy lives. Both of the sections spotlight what the tool is, why it should matter to you, how to implement the tool, and its cost. No matter the organizational structure and climate that we work in, these tools can activate our abilities to walk alongside, through, and past the chronic stress and vicarious trauma that is part of our profession. Some disciplines that inform the priorities of the nonprofit sector refer to the use of tools for this purpose as *harm reduction strategies.* Unmitigated chronic stress and vicarious trauma is *harm.* Mitigating chronic stress and vicarious trauma does not mean prevent it; rather, mitigating refers to *reducing* the intensity, lengthiness, and fallout of the chronic stress and vicarious trauma that is part of nonprofit community-based social services work. Readers do not have to wait for the nonprofit sector to culturally shift its norms discussed earlier in this book. We can do some things to mitigate the negative impact of chronic stress and vicarious trauma.

Ultimately, the curated tools are done for you, the reader, with care and caution. In attempting to avoid cliché self-help activities that often reflect Eurocentric and hegemonic biases in healing only some types of bodies, the tools in this chapter will hopefully intrigue you for the contemporary science and cultural origins that inform them. Rigorous studies out of universities, the military, and medical centers share with us many excellent options and these details are shared in this chapter with the intention to translate the facts quickly so that the benefits and practicality of each tool is obvious.

Engaging the Tools

Cultural appropriateness, finances, and nods at compliance statistics are all important to consider when reading and reflecting on each of the 17 tools. With cultural appropriateness, it is important to know thy ancestral heritage and recognize one's household culture. When experimenting and adopting tools, the tools will be weaved into the readers' homes and those tools can be allied with routines and activities that already exist in daily life. For example, if a reader has an ancestral heritage practice that involves prayer or meditation on some repeating schedule (i.e., every Friday evening), then check out Tools #3 and #11; perhaps these can, like a flower, bloom alongside your existing practice by including creative ways to add the tools to what you already do. Further, if a reader has a household culture of Friday and Saturday night family movie nights with their school-age children, then check out Tools #5 and #12; perhaps these can be used while enjoying that household ritual.

Still further, finances should be considered when readers are engaging the 17 tools described in this chapter because if we are already spending money on health practices for other reasons, we may not have funds left to use with new resources. Some of the tools have costs associated with them, ranging $5 to $150, but the majority of the tools have no financial cost.

Finally, compliance research results and recommendations, research which focuses on how often various groups of people comply with an instruction or tool, can be interpreted in several ways. How about we, those of us who are committed to finding ways to mitigate the chronic stress and vicarious trauma in nonprofit community-based social services jobs, agree to interpret compliance/noncompliance issues in the following way? How about we commit to ourselves that with reading each of the tools in this chapter, we will consider how well the tool can weave into our lives, family's lives, financial responsibilities, and our private anguishes and hopes that permeate all that we do? Let's start out our experimentation with the tools in this chapter with full understanding that some tools will work for us and some will not. For those tools that do not weave into the many layers of our lives, that's fine; please treat yourself with grace. When a tool isn't a match, it means the tool or the presentation of the tool by me, the author, isn't right at this point. Please explore the 17 tools with curiosity about the ways that you can playfully activate them in your life even under the exhaustion of unmitigated chronic stress and vicarious trauma. After each set of tools, divided into *On the Go* and *A Bit More Time*, there are examples provided for you and templates that you can use to explore the individualistic and collective components of addressing unmitigated chronic stress and vicarious trauma.

On the Go

Tool 1: Images of Nature

What: Buy, print, or draw green and blue images to hang all over your office space. Surrounding one's self with images of nature positively impacts our biology by reducing our experience of stress. This tool is shown in many studies for addressing some of the negative impacts of chronic stress and vicarious trauma.

Why this tool is important: Dozens of studies illustrate the connection between natural scenery and improved health across mental, physical and social factors (Abraham et al., 2010; Finlay et al., 2015). Importantly, studies also show that we do not have to actually be in natural green and blue spaces such as forests and parks (Jo et al., 2019; van den Berg et al., 2015). If one lives in a place without access to safe parks and scenic outdoor environments, the measurable benefits to surrounding ourselves with imagery has been studied and published by researchers nearly 40 times. Further, the science helps us to understand that even as short as a 90-minute walk in a scenic space, should we be able to access such, makes positive impacts that even brain scans pick up on (Gregory et al., 2015).

How: Quickly scan images online, print a few that align with your personality or interests, pin them on the wall where you spend a lot of time, and bam, get back to your to do list. If you have a few extra minutes, purchase posters online or swing by a thrift store to scan their collection of framed art.

Cost: This tool is free if you print nature images from your home printer or draw with your home art supplies. There's a cost for ordering online or making a store purchase for large posters of nature images. Many of us love to talk with plants; if you can keep them alive, borrow plant clippings for no cost to spawn at your desk like the reliable pothos plant species.

Tool 2: Walking Meetings

What: Take work meetings to the sidewalk or park if the office is located in a safe space, weather permits, and outdoor air quality is appropriate. This might take multiple attempts to get one's self and colleagues used to leaving the chairs, PowerPoints, and handouts behind, but keep at it. In fact, if colleagues are promised a meeting free of handouts and PowerPoint, they may be easy converts.

Why this tool is important: Research shows that walking meetings, with and without supports like smart phone apps, show several positive outcomes for individuals and organizations. Some of the benefits include improved well-being and health as well as creativity and perceived productivity (Ahtinen et al., 2016; Oppezzo and Schwartz, 2014). While this is an "on the go" tool, allowing two to four colleagues at a time to literally be on the go, it takes forethought such as considering which discussion topics are best for walking meetings. Great discussion topics for walking meetings include brainstorming solutions to an existing problem or, as we saw earlier in this book, staff and supervisor one-on-one meetings. Even reviewing plans already developed for an event and reflecting on recently completed projects can be the focus of walking meetings.

How: There are two popular smart phone apps that are geared towards teams and effective walking meetings, *Statik* and *Beenote*. Importantly, mobility is a diverse experience; since there is little research on walking meetings in terms of the benefits and best practices for persons with physical mobility disabilities, check out a great resource by Beth Kanter at the Nonprofit Technology Conference (2018). Further, safety matters; is your team located in a place where walking meetings can safely occur outdoors? Finally, consider keeping a list called "Great Topics for Walking Meetings" which could serve as a repository of collectively agreed-upon standards for walking meetings. When creating the annual organizational calendar, make sure to indicate possible walking meeting "seasons," especially if there are only certain times of the year that allow for walking meetings.

Cost: This tool is free if you print all materials, like the "Great Topics for Walking Meetings" list, at your office.

Tool 3: Drink Water, Por Favor!

What: Drinking more water every day, getting ourselves out of moderate dehydration that is so common today, can increase great things like a strong working memory and alertness. Drinking more water every day can also decrease challenges associated with chronic stress and vicarious trauma like headaches, intense negative moods, and fatigue (Ganio et al., 2011; Price & Burls, 2015; Spigt et al., 2012).

Why this tool is important: In many cities, readers can access clean water through city investments and/or reverse osmosis options in bottles at grocery stores. Experimenting with this tool could be a means for many fast paced, talented nonprofit professionals to support their physical body across the course of their contributions to this sector. Many of us have been conditioned to work ourselves out of alignment with the needs and requests of our bodies.

How: Go with the approach called *increasing compliance* which means that you attach this tool to something else in your routine and/or environment in order to help yourself to increase your likelihood of success. For example, you might get a few water bottles and put your name on them so that colleagues don't adopt them and/or can help you locate the bottles as you leave them in your path. Fill up the water bottles and leave them everywhere that you are most likely to see and access the bottles: desk, car, bag, and home. Find the most ideal bottles or the least expensive options at discount stores, online during sale seasons, and even secondhand stores.

Cost: The cost for this tool comes from having one or more cool water bottles that you want to use. These run about $5 to $50 per bottle.

Tool 4: Sleep at 65 Degrees Fahrenheit

What: In order to get the best sleep possible within the amount of time that many nonprofit professionals have available, we must follow the science on sleep. Keeping our rooms around 65 to 72 degrees Fahrenheit is shown to support us in staying asleep.

Why this tool is important: Studies show that the human body undergoes insufficient sleep patterns in the temperature above or below 65 to 72 degrees Fahrenheit (Lan et al., 2019; Obradovich et al., 2017). The insufficiency also includes other unfortunate outcomes such as waking after a hot sleep with elevated levels of the stress hormone cortisol (Lan et al., 2017).

How: If you have an air conditioning unit and the finances to keep it at this temperature range during the warmest season, then definitely use this easy tool. You might also approach this tool with placing an ice pack in one's pillow case or even purchasing technologies that are available for placing under one's sheets, "cooling pads."

Cost: The cost for this tool varies, ranging from one-time costs of $5 to $70 for an ice pack or a "cooling pad." Ongoing costs could be challenging such as for long-term use of air conditioning. Cost also depends on geographic location, quality of the air conditioning unit, personal funds, and access to resources like "cooling pads."

Tool 5: Holding Hands and Embraces

What: Physical touch on the arms and hands can activate important chemicals in our bodies (i.e., oxytocin) that translate as peace, calm, and safety for most adults and children (Cascio et al., 2019; Field, 2010; Olausson et al., 2002). Within a consensual context and among the appropriate people, touching and receiving healthy and safe touch is an "On the Go" tool for those of us working in stressful settings.

Why this tool is important: Many studies illustrate the specific benefits of touch, including decreasing depressive symptoms, increasing attentiveness, decreasing pain, and even strengthening our immune systems (Field, 2010; Uvnäs-Moberg et al., 2014). The gains for using this tool remain even after the touch and/or embrace take place, particularly among children and youth. This tool will be relevant to all readers even once readers are no longer working in the nonprofit sector, hopefully due to retirement. When public crises occur such as pandemics and natural disasters, don't pass on this tool. That is, consider all of the ways that you can put it to use.

How: Find friends or family to hold your hand, squeeze your arm, or even embrace you on some sort of a regular basis. If this is way out of the realm of possibility for you, get a *weighted blanket* to drape around your body. Weighted blankets are now more mainstream than in the previous decade. These blankets can be found through quick internet searches and at local stores. Consider having one of these blankets at your office for your short lunch break and/or at home for your short meal times (i.e., I hope that you get more time for eating at your own home!).

Cost: The cost for this tool ranges. It is a free tool in terms of relying on physical connection with friends and family. However, the cost of a weighted blanket will depend on the size and weight that is desired, but can start at $15 at many stores.

Tool 6: Terpene Up!

What: Walking in wooded areas and/or applying high-quality spruce essential oil is a tool that is super sciencie! Terpenes are from specific trees and are also referred to as "forest aerosols" and "terpenoids" in the research literature (Gershenzon & Dudareva, 2007; Sang Cho et al., 2017). Terpenes are perceived by our human noses and their benefits are explored in tumor and brain studies. These studies help us to understand the usefulness of terpenes in an accessible form like going on a walk in a wooded area or applying an essential oil.

Why this tool is important: Many research studies reveal the tremendous benefits of terpenes for our bodies. For example, we could experience calming effects, antidepressant functions, and curb brain inflammation according to scientists who have and continue to explore the impact of terpenes (Alberti et al., 2017).

How: In Japan, people can get what amounts to a prescription to miss work and walk in the forest (Sang Cho et al., 2017). Ask your American-based primary care doctor … see how they respond! The rest of us can arrange a day every month to walk in a wooded area if we have geographic access to such an area and a flexible lifestyle. Even easier, purchase a high-quality spruce essential oil to keep in one's bag and apply to one's skin daily. Researchers have used the essential oils of Idaho Blue Spruce and Hinoki in their studies.

Cost: The cost for this tool could be free for some of us. However, access to wooded areas may require an entrance fee to a park of $5 to $10. Further, the purchase of a high-quality spruce essential oil is about $30, lasting about four to six weeks depending on the frequency of application.

Tool 7: Turn Down Blue Lights

What: As many readers know, light from natural and artificially produced sources is actually along a color spectrum. We may see a specific color associated with a lamp or light bulb, such as white or yellow, but the reality is that light exists along a spectrum of blues to reds. Blue lights align with daylight from the sun. When our bodies are exposed to blue light, it impacts the body's regulation of hormones that are for staying awake versus winding down towards the end of the day. It can take hours for the impact of blue light to fade and sleep hormones to kick in.

Why this tool is important: Science shows that blue lights in the evening time have several negative impacts on the human body, including preventing the body from releasing enough melatonin to start winding down at the end of the day, preparing the body for falling asleep and staying asleep (Phelps, 2008; Zerbini et al., 2018). Even more research shows that for some of us who get headaches and/or eye strain from too much blue light exposure from computer screens and fluorescent overhead lighting fixtures, reducing this blue light can help (Lin et al., 2017). Even more, managing mental illnesses such as manic bipolar episodes are shown to be supported with increasing amber lighting, colors on the red end of the light spectrum (Henriksen et al., 2014; Phelps, 2008). Notably, fire, such as fire pits and fireplaces, do not have the blue lights that tell our body that the sun is still up. Our ancestors did not have to outsmart technologies that emit blue light because there weren't these issues to contend with.

How: Free apps for your smart phone, laptop, tablet, and television allow for us to dim the blue light that is being emitted from these devises. For example, f.lux is a well-known application for laptops that can be programed to dim blue light at a specific time each day. Further, television settings can be managed to reduce blue light for those late-night movies. Also, there are two reputable brands of blue light blocking glasses. The company called BluBlox is out of Australia and has good customer service reviews and use research studies for the design of their glasses. The second company called TrueDark is in the U.S. and also has research findings backing their design of the glasses. Both of these brands show us their product third-party testing results and quality assurance practices that go into creating their glasses. Be aware that sometimes, some people have a transition period to watching television with software or glasses blocking some of the blue light. That is, you may find that it takes you two weeks until you stop being distracted that the television is not showing you the full range of colors in the movies that you are used to watching. Finally, swing by the hardware store and grab a few red lightbulbs; swap these into lamps for use at night to reduce exposure to blue lights in the home prior to bedtime.

Cost: The costs for this tool ranges. The free app and television settings are the easiest and free to implement. Quality and tested blue light blocking glasses are around $100 and red lightbulbs range from $10 to $40.

Tool 8: Laugh Your Ass Off

What: Laughter is shown to increase chemicals in our bodies that translate as experiencing happiness. Laughter can be brought on through interpersonal exchanges (i.e., a hilarious friend) as well as from sources like movies and stand-up comedy performances. Studies show us a lot about the biological usefulness of laughing, even its importance, as a tool to respond to chronic stress and vicarious trauma. Research studies show that laughter can decrease blood pressure and increase oxygen intake. Spontaneous and self-induced laughter are both options (Cai et al., 2014; Mora-Ripoll, 2010).

Why this tool is important: At many points in our jobs, nonprofit social service professionals already laugh. However, often this laughter is only momentary comic relief about a difficult experience with a client or a community harm issue that we try to take the edges off by using dark humor (Hatzipapas et al., 2017; Emmerson, 2018). Laughter as a coping mechanism in high stress work situations is legitimate. Yet, instead, this tool here, *Laugh Your Ass Off*, could support nonprofit community-based social services professionals with intentionally prompting our bodies to create a cascade of happy chemicals with short- and long-term effects. Studies educate us about this cascade of chemicals which provides short-term benefits like improving memory, improving depression, decreasing anxiety, and elevating our moods (Bains et al., 2015; van der Wal et al., 2019; Chang et al., 2013). Related studies also show us the ways that laughter provides long-term protective benefits such as, when combined with other tools, laughter can strengthen resilience (López-Fuentes et al., 2015). For example, the long-term impact of laughter includes the release of neuropeptides that can strengthen the immune system.

How: We can inject laughter into our routines in advance of grinding job tasks. For example, in the midst of a very long day, listen to funny content while driving to a community site visit. And, in the evening after we get the kids off to bed, watch some stand-up comedy while cleaning the kitchen. The world of YouTube provides access to partial and full episodes of stand-up comedy performances and comedic movies. For those with subscriptions to content platforms like Netflix, Amazon Prime, and so forth, you can consume comedies over and over,

Cost: This tool is free on some platforms like YouTube and podcasts, but will include monthly fees for subscription platforms like Netflix.

Tool 9: Petting and Playing with Animals

What: Many people hear about the benefits of having a domesticated animal in one's life such as a pet dog or cat. Many more of us come from heritages that understand animals, including pets, as kin for which we share the earth and spirit worlds. Research studies confirm both the modern and ancient wisdom to stay connected to animals. The act of petting and/or spending time with dogs creates many benefits, including the reduction of distress among high-stress individuals and the creation of environmental supports that improve learning (Owen et al., 2016; Hall et al., 2016).

Why this tool is important: We may grumble as we feed our pets in the morning, itching to get everyone in the household taken care of before dashing off to focus on contributing to the precious lives of community members. Yet, right in front of many of us is an opportunity to reestablish important chemicals in our bodies that can serve us throughout the day.

Those puppy eyes are a signal to us to pause in order to nourish ourselves with this quick tool. Let those puppy eyes remind you of the gifts that our kin can offer us.

How: For those with pets in the home or on the property, here's what the science says: Having a dog in the home reduces likelihood of anxiety and distress, supports mental health, and increases one's self-esteem (Barcelos et al., 2020; Gadomski et al., 2015; Hawkins et al., 2019; Krause-Parello, 2012; Owen et al., 2016). Get started with short petting sessions. If you already cuddle your pet a few times each week, consider ways to increase the frequency. Also, consider volunteering a few hours a month to support sheltered animals. Engage your neighbor's dog with a yummy treat and a belly rub. Even try pet sitting for a friend who travels often.

Cost: Bringing a domesticated animal into the home can be costly, including wholesome food, biodegradable poop bags, toys, carpet shampooer, and so on. These costs will add up. However, the option of borrowing time with someone else's pet is free.

Tool 10: Brain Music

What: What is referred to as *neurologic music therapy* can positively impact our brains. Studies with persons with brain injuries show that such music can support us with retraining auditory perception, increasing our ability to focus, improve memory, and advance our problem-solving and decision-making (Hoemberg, 2005; Haslam & Cook, 2002; Ma et al., 2001; Impellizzeri et al., 2020; Thaut et al., 2009). Further, *neurologic music therapy* for just 30 minutes a day was found to support improved quality of life for people with chronic disease (Quach & Lee, 2017). Also amazing for our brains is drumming. Many studies show that drumming can decrease anxiety and stress and even increase the immune system functions (Bittman et al., 2001; Rojiani et al., 2021; Smith et al., 2014).

Why this tool is important: Listening to and/or singing along with certain types of music could help us with our daily grind. *Neurologic music therapy* is used as an evidence-based approach in an array of therapeutic spaces, including for the rehabilitation treatment post brain injuries referred to as *traumatic brain injuries* (TBI). While many of us do not experience TBIs nor chronic disease, healing sound frequencies from recordings and/or drumming are found to stimulate neuron reactions in regions of our brains that can support advancements around focus, memory, and so forth.

How: Accessing various types of music that fall under an umbrella

category of neurologic music is pretty easy. Once you have the music, you could choose from playing it as background music at your community center or office space, in the car or train during your commute, and at your residence.

Cost: There are three cost approaches to making this tool accessible to readers. First, some music therapy sources for benefiting the brain can be found for free on the internet. You may want to do a search for terms such as *neurological brain music* and *binaural beats*. You can then sort through options that you want to try out for yourself. Second, if you have a subscription to a music provider, you can search for music in your provider's supply with similar search terms. Third, those of us with ceremonial drums and supplies in our homes can use these supplies more often, translating the ceremonial purposes of our drums into daily ceremony opportunities.

Experimenting with On the Go Tools

Before we move on to read about the tools in *A Bit More Time*, Marcela, a caseworker in a community-based nonprofit organization serving teen parents, offers insights on how to start using the tools 1 through 10.

Marcela's Approach to Using On the Go Tools

Marcela knows that the teens and their kiddos at the center of her work take a significant amount of her mental space. She's perfectly okay with this fact; during the past three years in this role, serving the teens and their children has been truly in alignment with her career path and personal values. Hence, she engages selected tools from this chapter with both appreciation for the clients and for her body's strength and health. While reading this book, and with a big pink pen, she marked two of the On the Go tools, including Terpene Up! *and* Images of Nature.

Marcela also programmed her calendar to remind her in two months to return to this book chapter. She wants to add a few more On the Go tools to her daily life and she is determined to add at least one of the A Bit More Time tools described below. That is, Marcela plans to remain in nonprofit community-based social services organizations for decades to come, yet she already feels the weight of the last few years on her body. Low energy, complaining a lot, and difficulty feeling excited about her work are warning signs for her that practical tools like those featured in this book are what she needs.

*Marcela knows that drinking more water—*Drink Water, Por Favor!*—is a lost cause for her. She's tried that for years! She skipped right past that tool! However, she quickly ordered a high-quality spruce tree essential oil from a family member who sells high quality essential oils. Since it arrived in the mail, she keeps it in her bag and dabs it on her wrists three to five times a day. She's all about smelling like a spruce tree and* Terpene Up!

Marcela had been meaning to beautify her work cubicle and, ultimately, reading about the tool called Images of Nature *lit a fire under her to add green nature pictures to her cubicle. She used the color printer at the offices, printing four pictures and placing them in 10×7 frames that she had in a closet at home. These framed pictures along with two large posters ordered online surround her; when she's not meeting with teens and their children, she looks around her cubicle walls at the natural scenery.*

In the near future, Marcela will be back to this chapter to add more On the Go tools and at least one of the A Bit More Time tools.

A Bit More Time

Tool 11: Loving-Kindness

What: Loving-Kindness is a well-studied 12- to 15-minute compassion-focused meditation that can create several short- and long-term benefits to counter the fallout of chronic stress and vicarious trauma.

Why this tool is important: Studies show that there are short- and long-term health benefits to using the Loving-Kindness meditations, including increasing the daily presence of positive emotions (Fredrickson et al., 2017), improving relationships, decreasing distress, and increasing positive thinking (Shonin et al., 2014). Even after only one six-hour training and two follow-up evening meditation activities, people who use a Loving-Kindness meditation can cope better when facing new instances of distress from other people (Klimecki et al., 2013).

How: Meditation research centers, such as University of California Berkeley's Greater Good Science Center, provide free tools to the public. Visit this Center's website to find a Loving-Kindness guided meditation and clear instructions. Find a location and time of day where there are no disruptions for about 15 minutes. Plug headphones into a laptop, tablet, or smart phone, and follow the guided meditation.

Cost: This tool is entirely free if you already have a handheld device and headphones.

Tool 12: Outsmart Clutter

What: Did you know that clutter, even if it is a longstanding personality trait, distracts the mind's focus and creates added stress on the brain? Researchers identify several negative things that come from cluttered spaces in the home and/or office, including increased mental stress, barriers to managing existing post-traumatic stress, and overall dulled alertness (Khanade et al., 2018; McMains & Kastner, 2011). This tool is all about moving the clutter out of one's view and/or changing one's clutter-related habits. Some readers have secretly wished for a good reason to change this area of their life; here you are.

Why this tool is important: Long-term, studies show that doing nothing about the clutter in your spaces decreases life satisfaction inside and outside of the office (Dao & Ferrari, 2020; Crum & Ferrari, 2019; Ferrari et al., 2018).

How: This tool can be implemented in several ways. One approach is to focus on adjusting clutter-related habits by getting bins for under tables and beds, designated drawers for sweeping those things sitting on surfaces out of sight, and/or going vertical with items placed in closets. Another approach is to simply get things out of sight. The science doesn't say that we have to clear out closets! An option is to fill up those closets so that you don't have to see the clutter! Another option is to "Marie Kondo" the hell out of the workspace. Read one of Ms. Kondo's short books or watch interviews with her online to learn about the mindset she champions for clearing your spaces. The third approach is definitely a much more time-consuming way to go.

Cost: This tool ranges from free to about $100 worth of organizing bins. Depending on where you find these bins, that's your cost. Consider bins from local secondhand stores or shipping boxes that you typically put in your residential recycling bin. Also, for $12, buy one of Ms. Kondo's books which can walk the reader through her process.

Tool 13: Tension & Trauma Release Exercise

What: Tension & Trauma Release Exercise (TRE) was founded more than 20 years ago by Dr. David Berceli, Ph.D., a social worker and counselor by training. He created a science-based solution to move stress and trauma-related tension out of the body. TRE is a series of stretches and muscular engagements that target communication with the nervous system to allow the body to tremor (i.e., shake). The shaking is the mechanism for releasing tension. Hang tight with the idea of voluntarily shaking ... see the research below. Importantly, Dr. Berceli started TRE with refugee populations and the U.S. military, two groups of people who carry a lot of tension in their bodies related to high stress contexts. Cultural studies of African societies such as Namibia and Botswana as well as North American societies in the most northern regions illustrate the central practice of shaking for healing and ceremonial purposes (Keeney, 2004; Keeney, 2007; Struthers & Eschiti, 2005).

Why this tool is important: Several studies, both mammalian and human specific, illustrate the prevalence of shaking to release tension in the body following stressful events (Berceli et al., 2014; Harrison et al., 2018; Payne & Crane-Godrea, 2015; Swann, 2019; Wasserman, 2017). In human studies, some types of stressful events do not have to occur in real time to bring the body into a stressed and tense state; that is, even imagining and replaying stressful events activate stress hormones and the biological reactions such as restricting blood flow to organs (e.g., traumatic events like a gun shooting, an escape from a mugger, or a car crash). Imagining and replaying stressful events can raise adrenaline for alertness and diminish the use of the frontal lobe in order to pause analytical skills and emphasize the ancient part of the human brain for fighting, fleeing, or freezing to withstand the stressful event (Dzubur, 2017; Figley, 2006; Wasserman, 2017). Today, TRE is used by Certified TRE Practitioners who are social workers, therapists, and various types of body workers (e.g., massage therapists). Once a person learns how to do TRE from a Certified TRE Practitioner, how to implement the TRE process, the tool is self-sufficient. After one training, a person no longer needs to rely on a Certified TRE Practitioner. This is one of Dr. Berceli's greatest contributions: Giving us a healing modality that does not require a professional on more than one occasion.

How: Avoid the American temptation to xenophobia. This long-time practice is only seemingly exotic or foreign to those who are far removed from the diversity of healing modalities around the globe and across linear time. Visit www.traumaprevention.com to locate a Certified TRE Practitioner nearby in order to learn the TRE process. Some Certified TRE Practitioners remotely facilitate the TRE process through online video conferencing. Dr. Berceli also published a book with the process and, spurred by the COVID pandemic, made a free instructive video that might still be available on the website. Overall, plan to be available for an hour to an hour and a half to learn the TRE process. Further, if you come from kin who utilize shaking, perhaps you will want to invest time in growing your relationship and understanding of this gift.

Cost: The cost can be free with Dr. Berceli's 2020 online instructive video. Also, for $14, the book by Dr. Berceli is available. And, depending on the city in which you live, you can partner with a Certified TRE Practitioner for $80 to $100 in order to learn the process with direct support.

Tool 14: Expand Influence

What: An *expander* is a person who displays some or all of the qualities or activities that one desires to have in their own lives and, importantly, looks and appears similar to one's self. The expander communicates what is possible for one's self in terms of accessing those same, idealized qualities or activities. Hence, this American pop culture term refers to a person being *expanded* by seeing someone who shares similarities to them, though the expander has already accessed the desired ideals.

Why this tool is important: Studies of the subconscious show that parts of our brains operate like recording systems that replay and loop patterned thoughts and images that were programed or socialized into it, usually, long ago (Gustafson, 2017; Mulder, 2007; Sweatt & Sweatt, 2013). There's no sweet-talking the subconscious to adopt new programs. Nope. There must be repetition of new patterned thoughts and images to replace the previous looping patterns (Land et al., 2016; Yao et al., 2013). To alter the patterns and images, studies show that we must introduce new thoughts and images across time that leads to changes in our behavior, a reset of sorts. Hence, consistent exposure to expanders via recorded videos, audiobooks, etc., can offer us new thoughts and images that can replace our current patterns, informed by expanders who our subconsciouses recognize as being similar to us.

How: Tool 14 requires attention on a regular basis. Start by listening to videos and podcast interviews with specialists such as Dr. Joe Dispenza and Dr. Bruce Lipton. These researchers have several books and hundreds of freely available interviews in which they explain the science and solutions to swap in new patterned thoughts and images. *Expanders* must resonate with the readers in some form in order for us to create a connection or attachment to the expander and their expansive examples. For instance, consider someone who shares your demographics or life experience, yet is demonstrating the idealized qualities or activities that you're desiring. Some of the expanders that I engage through online videos and books include Selma Hayek, Eva Longoria, Michelle Alexander, and Oprah Winfrey. Each of these expanders have similar upbringings to me, have parallel parenting and societal pressures, and engage comparable reform interests as me. My subconscious can see their similarities. All four of these women also display idealized qualities or activities that become more possible to my subconscious, according to the research, when I ensure repeated exposure to their content.

Cost: The cost for this tool is free in terms of accessing online video interviews and lectures with the doctors listed above. Free public library content is also an option for readers. For books by the doctors as well as your own expanders, expect to pay $20–30 per book.

Tool 15: Lay Like an "L"

What: Make a little bit of time to do a single yoga pose where you lay on your back and lift your legs up to rest on a wall, making your body appear like an "L" where the legs are the lengthiest part of the "L." This is historically called Viparita Karani in yoga traditions. While you and your colleagues may look strange to those unfamiliar with the science, here is permission to implement the "L" even at the office.

Why this tool is important: Studies show that once in the "L" position, the movement of blood and other fluids to the feet is significantly slowed, which can improve chronic inflammation and chronic pain in the lower half of our bodies (Bower et al., 2012; Hennard, 2011; Rajbhoj et al., 2015). The blood, and substances carried in the blood, become increased in the torso area of one's body. Studies also show improvement with such things as decreasing fatigue and improving mood, and overall improved quality of life (Bower et al., 2010; Cramer et al., 2017). Ultimately, the science illustrates that calming chemicals are increased in our bodies when the "L" position is used and practitioners across types of yoga traditions tend to recommend around 15 minutes in this pose.

How: Figure out a 15 minute or more pause in your weekly schedule for the "L" position. Locate a soft carpeted area or roll out a cozy yoga mat to lay on. Where one places one's feet, try not to scuff up the wall (i.e., perhaps remove shoes). Viola!

Cost: As long as readers already have or can borrow a yoga mat, this tool is free.

Tool 16: Chant

What: Chanting, repeating a specified phrase over and over, may be familiar to you. Those of us who come from cultural backgrounds where spiritual or religious chanting is part of our upbringing, we've witnessed or engaged in chanting. Sometimes chanting is done in combination with other repetitive activities like drumming, Tao calligraphy, dancing, holding beads, etc. Sometimes, chanting is done while sitting with one's eyes open or closed. Ultimately, there are many traditions that researchers have studied that show us the physical benefits of chanting for our bodies.

Why this tool is important: Studies on chanting show that we can experience increased blood flow in areas of the brain that create peacefulness and soothing experiences (Khalsa et al., 2009) and research subjects who engage in chanting can improve their overall quality of life after one month of implementation (Hudoba et al., 2019). And good news: Researchers report chanting meditations are one of the easier "treatments" to study because the chants are typically easy for the masses to learn, use, and remember.

How: Of the many chanting options, readers might find two traditions easily accessible online or in your current city. First, a Kundalini Yoga meditation that is often an introductory meditative chant has the user repeat the following phrase over and over in a steady stream: Sa-Ta-Na-Ma. There is a significant history to this chant and its use. Hence, be sure to look up this history when you can by visiting the Kundalini Research Institute at kundaliniresearchinstitute.org or visit their headquarters in New Mexico. Second, the well-known Nichiren Buddhist school chant that is the central practice has the user repeat the following over and over in a steady stream: Nam-myo-ho-ren-ge-kyo. Like with the Kundalini Yoga chant, there is deep scholarship and spirituality surrounding this chant; be sure to invest time for researching this tradition when you can by looking up the international organization called the Soka Gakkai International which likely has a chapter in your city. You can gain more insights at sgi-usa.org or by visiting their headquarters in California.

Cost: Chanting is free in terms of accessing video or audio examples of these two chanting traditions. You can find guidance on both chants online.

Tool 17: Inserting Needles

What: Inserting hair-thin needles into precise places in the body is a longstanding Chinese healing practice. It dates back to as early as 6,000 years ago (White and Ernst, 2004). The places on the body where certi-fied and trained Acupuncturists place the needles were developed across the history of this healing modality. More recently, acupuncture has been studied to understand the mechanisms at play that helps the Western world to legitimize this ancient healing practice.

Why this tool is important: In laboratory settings, researchers can detect some of the mechanisms that create pain relief when needles are placed at specific points on the body (Ahsin et al., 2009; Wang et al., 2013). In other mammal studies, we learn that the use of acupuncture can prevent animals from relapsing with narcotics when under stress (Yoon et al., 2012). Importantly, acupuncture use is found to positively impact research subjects by addressing stress and anxiety (Kim et al., 2009).

How: To find a professional that you're interested in working with, read the review feedback from users of Acupuncturists in your area and/or look for Acupuncturists listed in your medical insurance service pro-vider listing. Make the appointment anytime of the day. In order to insert the hair-thin needles in many relevant places on your body, plan to work with a professional who you are comfortable getting undressed with partially or fully. Depending on the intended outcomes of working with the Acupuncturist, you may not need to undress and only receive needles in areas like your hands and ears. Give it a go if you can afford this tool.

Cost: Typically, a visit to the Acupuncturist can range from $85 to $150. Be sure to call and talk about the cost before you schedule an appointment. Major medical establishments have Acupuncturists on their campuses and numerous types of medical insurance approve of a set num-ber of visits to an Acupuncturist per year.

Experimenting with
A Bit More Time Tools

Before we move on to the final sections of this chapter, Sebastián, an intake facilitator in a community-based nonprofit organization serving male residents at a temporary housing facility, offers insights on how he started using the tools that take *A Bit More Time*.

Sebastián's Approach to Using A Bit More Time *Tools*

Sebastián is ready to start working with new and returning residents at 7:30 a.m. every morning and stops only once during the day for a 20-minute lunch and very occasional bathroom breaks. He doesn't really mind the steady and consuming pace of tasks that spread across his entire day because he understands that the men he serves face significant challenges that he gets to help to resolve. He equally worries, however, about how long he will work at his current pace in this job. With a mechanical pencil in hand, he explores this chapter while waiting at the gas pump for his car gas tank to fill. He puts check marks next to Inserting Needles *and* Tension & Trauma Release Exercise.

Over and over, Sebastián returns to this chapter and his penciled notes in order to consider the current state of his health, the pace of his work life, and how these tools might help him to mitigate the negative impact of chronic stress and vicarious trauma. He finds acupuncture to be interesting and when first reading about the tool Inserting Needles, *he was surprised to see that studies exist that can help readers to understand some of the mechanisms at work for creating the beneficial outcomes of acupuncture treatments. One Sunday evening, he spent a lot of time exploring the American Society of Acupuncturists, checking out the resources and used the "Find a Practitioner" button to identify who he would call in the morning to schedule an appointment.*

At night, Sebastián sees the Netflix recommendations and YouTube ads that pop up on his TV referring to health and wellness trends, but Sebastián's not drawn to these. He does, however, sit down to read the website for Tension & Trauma Release Exercise *and later in the week he is planning to test out the free instructional video from the TRE website. Depending on how the instructional video goes for him, he might look up a local TRE Certified Practitioner to double check whether or not he is using this tool correctly.*

In the near future, Sebastián plans to turn back through the pages of this book to add more tools to his daily life. For now, he is confident that the two tools he selected so far are doable for his fast-paced life.

Closing

Marcela selected two of the On the Go tools with intensions to return to this chapter in the near future. Specifically, she programmed a calendar alarm to call out to her in a few months in order to remind her to reopen this book chapter and implement a few more tools. Marcela is practical. She shows readers how easily she put to use the On the Go tools. For those who learn and implement differently from Marcela, below is a checklist to support implementation of the tools in this chapter. Sebastián, however, was drawn only to the A Bit More Time tools. He jumped into looking up the two tools that he was most intrigued by, did some of his own user testing with

Tension & Trauma Release Exercise, and scheduled appointments with certified professionals for this tool and the one called *Inserting Needles.*

A spirit of experimentation is powerful, but so too is knowing that your exposure to chronic stress and vicarious trauma is not individually created nor individually solved. There are push and pull forces inside and outside of nonprofit community-based organizations. These forces are intentionally stifling to the missions of community-based organizations. These forces, principally racist and classist agendas, distract attention from fundamentally resolving the need for nonprofit professionals like you. Racist and classist agendas draw our attention to keeping the doors to our organizations open and triaging eminent threats to our precious community members. Many talented professionals, like you and your colleagues, inside community-based organizations, cannot look away from the eminent threats long enough to also mitigate the negative impact of chronic stress and vicarious trauma stemming from your organization not having mitigating mechanisms surrounding your job role. So ... use the tools in this chapter to support how you walk through your professional life even knowing that you, the individual, is not the solution to the problem central to this book's discussion.

On the Go

Which tools will I experiment with?

_____

- ☐ Tool 1: *Images of Nature*
- ☐ Tool 2: *Walking Meetings*
- ☐ Tool 3: *Drink Water, Por Favor!*
- ☐ Tool 4: *Sleep at 65 Degrees Fahrenheit*
- ☐ Tool 5: *Holding Hands and Embraces*
- ☐ Tool 6: *Terpene Up!*
- ☐ Tool 7: *Turn Down Blue Lights*
- ☐ Tool 8: *Laugh Your Ass Off*
- ☐ Tool 9: *Petting and Playing with Animals*
- ☐ Tool 10: *Brain Music*

A Bit More Time

Which tools will I experiment with?

_____

- ☐ Tool 11: *Loving-Kindness*
- ☐ Tool 12: *Outsmart Clutter*

☐ **Tool 13:** *Tension & Trauma Release Exercise*
☐ **Tool 14:** *Expand Influence*
☐ **Tool 15:** *Lay Like an "L"*
☐ **Tool 16:** *Chant*
☐ **Tool 17:** *Inserting Needles*

Assessing Your Experimentation

There are two easy ways for readers to consider whether or not any of the tools work for you. Use one or both of the following approaches.

Assessing Tool Impact, Approach 1

Explore the tools' alignment with your current routines, rituals, and so forth. Ask and answer the following for each tool with which you want to experiment:

1. Did I find ways to weave the tool into the cultural or religious aspects of my life? Did I ask confidants for feedback on how to do this weaving?

2. Was I thoughtful about how the tool and my finances intersect? Am I able to afford the tool if there is more than a one-time cost?

3. Did I find ways to add the tool to a routine or activity that I already do on a regular basis?

Reflections

_____

_____

_____

_____

Assessing Tool Impact, Approach 2

The second approach for assessing your experimentation with the tools and deciding how well the tools are jiving for you is to gather four types of information to then visually compare that information. Ask yourself clear questions about your life, family, financial responsibilities, and

118

private anguishes and ideals in order to see which tools are benefiting two, three, or four of these areas.

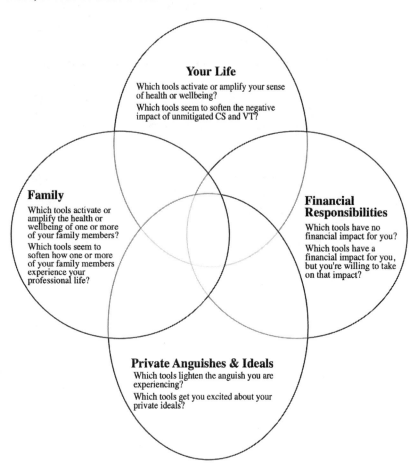

Your Life

Which tools activate or amplify your sense of health or wellbeing?

Which tools seem to soften the negative impact of unmitigated CS and VT?

Family

Which tools activate or amplify the health or wellbeing of one or more of your family members?

Which tools seem to soften how one or more of your family members experience your professional life?

Financial Responsibilities

Which tools have no financial impact for you?

Which tools have a financial impact for you, but you're willing to take on that impact?

Private Anguishes & Ideals

Which tools lighten the anguish you are experiencing?

Which tools get you excited about your private ideals?

It can be easy to select healing tools at the individual level that assist you in navigating unmitigated CS and VT in professional spaces by considering four areas that any tool might benefit.

Reflections

_____

_____

_____

_____

Chapter 5

Organizational Level Tools

Let us consider four cascading questions about nonprofit community-based social services organizations and the widespread lack of mitigation strategies for curbing the negative impact of chronic stress and vicarious trauma. The questions assist readers in considering the practical role that organizations play in supporting their staff team's lives. While the tools and support in this chapter are for the organizational leaders to implement, no matter your job role this chapter will assist you in processing the interplay of responsibilities for mitigating chronic stress and vicarious trauma at the individual, organizational, and sector levels. The questions include the following:

1. What are the stated organizational values listed on the organization's website?
2. Are these values intended to be community facing only?
3. If the stated values are also intended to be inward facing for application with the organizational team, can all coworkers recall the organizational values and/or point to ways the values are implemented within the organization and affect them?
4. Whether or not the stated values are community facing only, what submerged values lay beneath the surface of the organizational culture?

Nonprofit community-based organizations typically list their values alongside their organizational missions within their communication materials, including websites, social media profiles, handouts, and so forth. Whether or not stated, all organizations, including for-profit companies and government agencies, house a set of values though sometimes the values stated are not the same as the values that lay just beneath the surface of the organizational culture. For example, a stated value may be *equity* and yet work-life integration for employees with young children is absent. Verbally, equity is celebrated, but the organizational culture enforces the practice of working around the clock frantically with most work assignments labeled as urgent. Hence, the value for coworkers is not equity for diverse lifestyles, but rather, the value for coworkers is *production*. Close your eyes and visualize a sweatshop.

Too harsh? Maybe. The cascading four questions are revisited in the next chapter and its description of forces at work inside and external to the nonprofit

> *Using the Tools*
>
> *None of these tools are intended as an add on to the existing organizational way of doing things, including the team's routines, speaking patterns, tools, activities, and unspoken expectations for "normal" behavior (i.e., the organizational culture).*

sector more broadly. Many nonprofit professionals do not want their organizations to simply pass the responsibility down the line, or pass the garment to the next sewing machine. As the employer, professionals want their organizations to help solve unmitigated chronic stress and vicarious trauma. If the organizational stated values are not at the forefront of coworkers' minds, it is likely that the organization is not blowing life into those intended values, is not implementing them.

This chapter focuses on 11 tools for organizations to use to mitigate the negative impact of chronic stress and vicarious trauma. These are practical tools. However, they are most effective when concretely backed by organizational leadership and resources are put behind the tools for the long haul. Yet, nonprofit community-based social services professionals benefit from this chapter no matter their leadership role. That is, one day, some readers will transform into organizational leaders, leaders in funding entities, and perhaps leaders in institutions that create the problems that nonprofits are fixing! Hence, just like with the previous chapter, readers get to learn about tools that they can experiment with and use across time, today and into the future. Use this chapter as a reference source throughout your career.

Invest in Tools

The purpose of this chapter is not to make better workers, producers, and sacrifices. *Mitigating* chronic stress and vicarious trauma means to repair the damage done to nonprofit professionals by the nonprofit sector cultural fixation on urgency and overwhelm. These white supremacist notions both birth the racist and classist agendas that nonprofits are working to resolve as well as the work context of unmitigated chronic stress and vicarious trauma. There is a lot of research that sheds light on what chronic stress and vicarious trauma is doing to professionals across several sectors. The pain endured up to this point should be at the forefront of readers' minds while learning about and implementing the tools in this chapter that are geared for the organizational level. For example, professionals who experience the combination of high demands, low discretionary power, and an imbalance between efforts and rewards have increased risk of heart disease and mental illness (Head et al., 2007). If these are not striking enough, here are several more facts to consider:

- Professionals who work 70 hours per week for years have weak connections in their prefrontal cortex and fail to down regulate from laboratory induced stressors (Golkar et al., 2014).
- Chronic and cumulative contact with vicarious trauma is linked to depression (Regehr et al., 2004).
- As much as 41 percent of professionals who serve stigmatized groups are known to take a leave of absence for health reasons (Phillips et al., 2012).

> *What Orgs Must Address*
>
> *Professionals who experience the combination of high demands, low discretionary power, and an imbalance between efforts and rewards have increased risk of heart disease and mental illness (Head et al., 2007).*

- Vicarious trauma can negatively impact professionals' long-term mental health, relationships, and worldview (Aparicio et al., 2013).
- Professionals' likelihood of developing coronary heart disease increases by 34 percent when facing high demands and low discretionary power (Steptoe et al., 2013).

Some of the above facts are known, or should be known, by the leadership of nonprofit community-based organizations. For example, when team members are working over 40 hours per week and frequently using sick days, organizational leaders are supposed to notice. Entire teams are drowning in the statistical data bullet pointed above. Nonetheless, there are several negative outcomes of unmitigated chronic stress and vicarious trauma that may go unnoticed such as medical diagnoses and chronic illnesses linked to the work culture that employees keep privately to themselves. Organizational leaders must move forward with the available facts, seeing this research as immediately relevant for protecting their teams.

Nothing in this book will ever argue that organizations will have more efficient and healthier workers if they implement science-backed tools. If efficiency and health are consequences of mitigating the negative

impact of chronic stress and vicarious trauma on the team of professionals, that's a great bonus. However, the title of this book, *Nonprofit Work is
Killin' Me*, reflects the state of work life for many of the professionals who
comprise nonprofit community-based social services organizations.

What Is the State of Your Team?

In the fall of 2018, as faculty at California State University Fresno,
I launched an anonymous electronic survey study with nonprofit professionals 18 years and older who were currently employees at nonprofit
organizations. This study was described earlier in this book, exploring
the nonprofit work experiences with attention to the rate of, and factors
involved in, chronic stress and vicarious trauma. The results of the study
contribute significantly to our understanding of what is happening in the
nonprofit sector and, more specifically, what is happening to nonprofit
professionals in social services job roles. Please return to the earlier discussion of these results.

Did you know that at the time of the 2018 study, there were no
university-based research studies on this topic as it pertains to nonprofit
community-based social service organizations? In the introduction of this
book, the limited research that is available on vicarious trauma in nonprofit organizations with social services was explained. Overall, there is
a historical dearth in exploring these things within direct service jobs
that are not formally designated as "therapist," "social worker," and so
forth (Baines, Hadley, & Slade, 2002; Holness et al., 2004). My study also
addresses this research gap. Further, in nonprofit management literature,
we see that, unfortunately, authors of those sources often conflate chronic
stress, compassion fatigue, vicarious trauma, and burnout which can
make results unclear and solutions difficult to identify. In my study, I was
careful to use survey tools that allow for distinguishing among chronic
stress, compassion fatigue, vicarious trauma, and burnout in order to have
a rigorous contribution to our nonprofit sector.

There were 73 survey respondents included in the study. Many gen-
erous professionals responded to the survey, though only those who were
employed full-time in nonprofit community-based social services organizations were included. Their demographic indicators were discussed in the
earlier chapter, but based on the data we can make a composite or ava-
tar in order to get a sense of what unmitigated chronic stress and vicarious trauma look like at the organizational team level. Respondents were

largely from California (77 percent). Based on the demographics, many teams working directly in the community, within community-based social services organizations, look like the following:

- Your team is likely comprised of professionals 18 to 50 years old, with the largest age group ranging 31 to 40 years old (29%).
- The professionals are mostly female identifying (73%).
- Almost all of the team stems from white heritage (71%), with the next likely heritage group being Latino.
- Finally, almost half of the composite team has spent three to nine years in community-based nonprofit organizations (46%).

The survey responses were analyzed and earlier discussed through the lens of individuals. Here, we have explored the demographic data at a composite team level. We will also do this same thing for the study results. Based on the study results surrounding unmitigated chronic stress, your team, who is working directly in the community, is likely exhausted:

- About half of your team is likely worn out at the end of each work day (52%).
- A significant portion of the professionals on your team feel exhausted in the morning at the thought of another day at work (33%).
- Your team has little energy remaining for family and friends (72%).
- About half of your team likely feels tired outside of workday hours (48%). More specifically, almost half of the professionals are physically exhausted outside of work hours (39%). And almost half are emotionally exhausted outside of the workday (43%).
- Dating to before the recent pandemic, about a third of your team is thinking "I can't take it anymore" (28%).

Further, based on the study results surrounding unmitigated vicarious trauma, your team is likely experiencing work-based vicarious trauma at significant rates.

- For solely supervisees, many on your team are likely experiencing vicarious trauma with scores ranged 13 percent to 24 percent on the vicarious trauma indicators listed below.
- For any of your team members who are directly serving community members, almost a third are thinking about distressing client/program participant issues outside of work (24%).

- And the same number of them feel helpless to assist their clients in the way that they would like to (24%).

For solely supervisees rather than those with supervising roles, 61 percent of them were working more than 40 hours per week for your organization. Organizational leaders must contend with this reality. It is neither reasonable nor sustainable to fail your team by not implementing mitigating mechanisms to curb chronic stress and vicarious trauma *and* work employees into overtime. The highlights bulleted above must be viewed as the likely situation of your organization's team; let this data motivate you to experiment with and adopt organizational tools presented in this chapter.

How to Implement Tools

There are at least two approaches that organizations can ride in order to implement their values. It is assumed that your organizational values are intended to affirm the well-being of a specific population. Turn those values inward towards your own team members.

The implementation approaches promoted here are not linear paths of guaranteed outcomes. The only guarantee is that using either of the two approaches with authenticity and commitment, will move your team from unmitigated chronic stress and vicarious trauma to a better state. Nonlinear and inclusive approaches to tool adoption will look messy to many team members. That is, whether your team is white or acculturated to white supremacy, the two approaches will not promote linear, step-by-step actions, timelines, and outcomes. Stated another way: "Professionalism has become the pseudonym for assimilation" (Rahim-Dillard, 2021). As your team selects Approach 1 or Approach 2 for your organization to prepare for experimenting with the tools below, Rahim-Dillard is helping us to understand that *messy* is often a description applied to non-white supremacist approaches and that to show or to be "professional" means to assimilate to white supremacist mannerisms such as linear, conflict-free, and comfortable approaches.

> *Implementation Approaches*
>
> *Replace, disrupt, alter, and/or re-alchemize the organizational culture without an official plan for doing so. Try out the tools and see what works.*

Your organizational boat will move downstream, across seas, and through oceans that otherwise your organization would not get to experience from a fly-over approach. A fly-over approach is not affirming of the well-being of your team members. Instead, this refers to surveying the available tools, pointing them out from the window of the airplane, and moving on. Perhaps in earlier internal initiatives that your organization has launched, a newsletter article about wellness tools or a special room was designated for de-stressing. These are bullshit fly-over approaches. In order to mitigate the negative impact of chronic stress and vicarious trauma that inundates organizational teams, viola, the purpose of this book; choose otherwise.

In order to prepare your organization for meaningful adoption of tools that can help to mitigate the negative impact of chronic stress and vicarious trauma, replace, disrupt, alter, and/or re-alchemize your organizational culture. Before actually experimenting with the tools, testing how the tools align with one's team, organizational leaders must commit to one of the following approaches. None of the 11 organizational tools are intended as *an add on* to the existing organizational culture, including the team's routines, speaking patterns, activities, and unspoken expectations for "normal" behavior. That is right. In order to mitigate the negative impact of chronic stress and vicarious trauma that is central to the organizational mission, the culture must be adjusted to elevate and advance wellness of the team members.

Importantly, compliance research studies often examine groups of professionals or groups of experimental subjects. Frequently, the study results depict these groups as failing in some way when noncompliance occurs. Yet, what if the study asked, again, cascading questions about what came before the current compliance topic and what is the future constellation of practices that we are interested in reaching?

To work with an example from the previous chapter, when Australian and U.S. hospital workers do not comply with handwashing mandates 100 percent of the time (or even 90 percent), the questions revolve around How can compliance be increased? With nonprofit community-based organizations, what if we ask questions like these:

- Which tools or initiatives implemented in the past created tool or initiative fatigue for the professionals who comprise this team?
- How can the answers to this question be used to inform how we experiment with the tools in this chapter?
- What is the constellation of practices that we are interested in reaching to mitigate chronic stress and vicarious trauma among our professionals and how much of this constellation do we want to see by when?

Finally, finances should be considered when experimenting with the 11 organizational tools because if the organization is either already spending money on health and wellness practices for other initiatives or expecting employees to pick up the tab, the organizational leadership and its team must reroute funds to one of the curated tools in this chapter. In the contemporary U.S. context, putting money behind an organizational practice often communicates commitment. Note that six of the 11 tools have costs associated with them aside from staff time for implementation. Nearly all of the tools presented below have guides, checklists, and tips.

Approach 1: Cultural values must mirror the team's needs.

For riding this first wave, as the organizational leader, choosing this approach includes assuming that your organization intends for its values to serve the community *and* be turned inward towards the professionals inside of the organization. The organizational leadership and its team must confirm that the stated and implicit organizational values mirror the team's needs as the team fulfills the organizational mission. Recall from our earlier discussion of the nonprofit sector culture and norms, *values* are the same thing as saying *cultural values*. The stated and implicit organizational values reflect the organization's culture, and vice versa. For instance, with the survey study described above, the composite team based on the study findings reflects an organization with implicit values focused on white supremacy. That is, the Eurocentric industrial overworking of populations (i.e., working your staff team over 40 hours as well as cheap sweatshop labor like dynamics) and the lack of support (i.e., failure to mitigate chronic stress and vicarious trauma) has been with the Western industrial world for centuries. The white supremacy focus within an organization assumes natural and inevitable that staff teams must exhibit efficiency, individualism, fear of conflict, defensiveness, and urgency (Okum, n.d.). The white supremacy values are not able to support your organizational mission that, in some way, centers on community well-being for two reasons. First, with white supremacy values, the organizational team will exhibit the blowback described above from unmitigated chronic stress and vicarious trauma. Second, as discussed earlier in this book about the racist and classist foundation of the U.S. nonprofit sector culture, white supremacy values cannot dismantle the micro nor macro experiences of racism. Since the late 20th century to today, we have this gift to keep chewing on: "The master's tools will never dismantle the master's house" (Lorde, 1979).

Ask these three questions about the alignment between the stated and implied organizational values and team composition:

- Are the values culturally appropriate for the team members, reflecting their heritage and family values, as they strive to accomplish the organizational mission?
- Do the values amplify the gifts that the team members bring with them to the work place?
- Do the values frame the professionals as more than workers and producers for the organization and/or its funders, including seeing your team as members of families, caregivers, tax payers, weekend athletes, and so forth?

As discussed elsewhere in this book, nonprofit sector culture and norms will always impact what goes on inside of your organizational team; this is sometimes good and other times terrible (i.e., racism and classism). While assessing the stated organizational values with the three questions above, remember that there are certainly cultural values inside of your organization that are not official or listed anywhere, but that are prominent features in the daily activities of your team. Answering and resolving the three questions above must take place before experimenting with the organizational tools curated below. As organizational leadership, you have control over whether or not the organization's cultural values are inviting and supportive of tools that can mitigate the negative impact of chronic stress and vicarious trauma among the staff team. All of the tools available below do not align with white supremacy values.

Once your organization is ready to test out tools because your team has ensured alignment between the cultural values and team members, and ensured some form of coercion to make sure the values are consistently championed, the weaving of tools into your organization can commence. The tools, at the testing and full adoption stages, will be weaved into the lives of the team members and will eventually impact every department and unit. The tools should be coupled to routines, activities, and tasks that already exist in each department and unit. This way, the new tools can act as protective features against unmitigated

> *Professionals as Producers*
>
> *The contemporary dominant cultural narrative in the U.S. explicitly and implicitly extracts aspects of our lives and says that those aspects are less important. The parts that are allowed to remain unquestioned and valued are the parts that make us workers and producers.*

chronic stress and vicarious trauma that unfolds in the seeming mundaneness of the routines, activities, and tasks.

Recall that there is no linear and assured recipe to establishing new tools within an organizational culture because the organization and its team is encompassed by the larger contemporary U.S. dominant culture that overwhelmingly enforces racist and classist narratives that equate professionals to producers rather than treating professionals as full human beings. Getting your organization's cultural values appraised takes time and is also central to success with tool adoption. The tools that your team chooses to fully adopt will be vulnerable to being coopted by whatever cultural values that your organization holds.

Approach 2: The organization must explore which tools collectively benefit the team across four areas.

The second approach is an alternative to the first approach and includes a framework similar to that which was first introduced in the previous chapter which was focused on tools for the individual level. With Approach 1, organizations do not need to hire a consultant to do exploratory mission and vision exercises that most of us actually hate. As a friend recently stated, "I'd prefer a tooth extraction without pain meds." Likewise, with Approach 2, organizations can choose to go for a ride that looks more familiar to Eurocentric assessment approaches without the needs for an external consulting coach.

The approach here also helps your organization to prepare for the adoption of tools with consideration of the collective experience of the organizational team. This allows for your team to immediately begin experimenting with how well tools are jiving across the four concentric circles below. Unlike Approach 1, your team can jump in with Approach 2, but must maintain attention to experimenting with tools and returning frequently to the activities in Approach 2. The concentric circles allow your team to imagine the long-term outcomes for adopting any one tool. However, Approach 2 is also not linear, as with Approach 1. Experimenting with tools includes pausing to ask and reflect on the questions within the concentric circles.

The organizational team must collectively ask clear questions about the team's experiences with team well-being, responsibilities outside of the work day, organizational financial resources, and workplace anguishes and ideals. The collective inquiry in these four areas allows the team to explore which tools are benefiting two, three, or four of these areas and for how many of the team members.

While seeing your team members as full human beings and a magnificent collective of possibilities, attempt to select the best tools for mitigating the negative impact of chronic stress and vicarious trauma. Be wary, however, that your organization's cultural values can disable the positive impact of the tools. Keep an eye out for this. Without the accomplishments of Approach 1, stay suspicious of the ways that your organization welcomes, embraces, and supports or aggresses, micromanages, and opposes the tools.

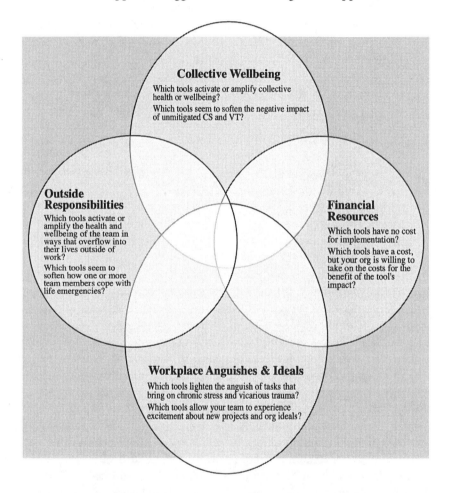

Collective Wellbeing

Which tools activate or amplify collective health or wellbeing?

Which tools seem to soften the negative impact of unmitigated CS and VT?

Outside Responsibilities

Which tools activate or amplify the health and wellbeing of the team in ways that overflow into their lives outside of work?

Which tools seem to soften how one or more team members cope with life emergencies?

Financial Resources

Which tools have no cost for implementation?

Which tools have a cost, but your org is willing to take on the costs for the benefit of the tool's impact?

Workplace Anguishes & Ideals

Which tools lighten the anguish of tasks that bring on chronic stress and vicarious trauma?

Which tools allow your team to experience excitement about new projects and org ideals?

Diagram 5.1 Approach 2 for priming your organization for tool adoption. At the team level, it can be easy to select tools for navigating and mitigating CS/VT in professional spaces by considering four areas that influence your team's experiences and organization.

Reflections

- How many members of the team positively benefit from the tool within each concentric circle?
- Of those team members who did not experience positive experiences, why is this?
- Majority benefit is not collective benefit. If no tool positively benefits every member of the team in at least two of the concentric circles, consider engaging Approach 1.
- Which circles are team members more frequently injured in your organizational context by the unmitigated chronic stress and vicarious trauma?
- Which circles are team members more drawn to discuss and want to keep tracking tool implementation for?
- Does the current organizational culture create a taboo around addressing one or more of the concentric circles?
- If so, will the implementation of tools that positively impact those circle(s) be sabotaged by the organizational culture? For example, are there routines, speaking patterns, tools, activities, and unspoken expectations for "normal" behavior that will obstruct authentic and complete implementation of the tool(s)?

What ideas and possibilities emerge from your team?

_____
_____
_____
_____

Collective reflection is needed when selecting the tools to test out and when assessing the relevancy of the tools for the team. Facilitated group discussions sorted by department, unit, role, age, cultural heritage, etc., can be the way that your organization engages Approach 2. Again, like with Approach 1, there is no need for an organization to hire a consultant to accomplish Approach 2. However, depending on the degree of white supremacy values that your organization maintains and any degree of denial about this, then hiring a consultant specialist in anti-racist and decolonizing practices can benefit your team's experimentation and adoption of tools. Remember that there is no separation between the existence of unmitigated chronic stress and vicarious trauma and racism and classism. These go together in the nonprofit sector.

Riding this wave is going to be challenging, but worth it for the purpose of transforming our society by transforming our nonprofit organizations and sector. Hiring a consultant to support your Approach 2 experience does not ensure that white supremacy values and possible denial about this state are going to be overcome. In fact, forgoing a consultant and allowing your team to get real with the state of unmitigated chronic stress and vicarious trauma at the intersection of racism and classism inside of your organizations is a humbling opportunity to do transformation. Organizational leaders must be ready for their personal fragility in terms of leaders who are white, male, and intentionally or unintentionally reinforce white supremacy values. While not an organizational level tool, such leaders will benefit from studying and traveling through the journey of the books *White Fragility* (DiAngelo, 2018) and *Nice Racism* (DiAngelo, 2021).

Tools

Your nonprofit community-based organization is going to run how it's going to run. This is not a defeatist statement. Whether you, the reader, are a staff member delivering direct services to community members or you find yourself in a role with a high degree of discretionary power, organizations are living organisms that are not likely to change quickly in the current Eurocentric climate. There is no need to wait for the *best* timing or a future benchmark in order to start changing the state of vicarious trauma and chronic stress experienced by your team.

The tools presented below are outlined much like the previous chapter; readers can quickly identify the what, why, how, and cost of each tool. Two things are particularly different about studying, reflecting on, and implementing organizational level tools versus individualized tools. First, there is only so much pressure that can be used across the team to ensure commitment to tool implementation. If you do not have a leading role in the organization, you can introduce the tool, advocate for its implementation, and so forth, but you may not have a leadership who is willing. That's expected in, again, organizations holding tight to white supremacist values.

The second thing to consider about organization level tool implementation is that one cannot implement a tool from this chapter and then be done. No tool is a one time thing. No pat on the back is waiting on the other side of an implemented team-based tool. No new, radical, and life-affirming work environment is unveiled on the other side of an implemented tool. The chosen tools will be implemented and then attention must be paid to their maintenance, the ways that the tools contend with changing team dynamics, and, when appropriate, the retirement of past tools for new tools.

Also, using a tool from this chapter is much like any other organizational level initiative or major investment. No matter the tool, a majority of team members must value and maintain the tool, and hence, ensure the tool's ongoing relevance. Like your organization's van, let's say, for picking up and dropping off children and teens on programming days, ask yourselves whether the van's engine fluids are maintained, seatbelts checked for functionality (i.e., seatbelt replacements can cost about $1000), and whether the van is lice free from the kiddo who brought little friends to the program. This is the same attentiveness that must be applied to organizational level tools for mitigating the negative impact of chronic stress and vicarious trauma among your team.

Tool 1: Unionize Your Nonprofit

What: Employee-directed nonprofit organizations can equip the team with collective leadership practices to organize the team's work in ways that mitigate chronic stress and vicarious trauma. This tool promotes learning more about unionizing and training opportunities in order to understand the many benefits that research studies show about such a model (Mananzala & Spade, 2008).

Why this tool is important: With the implementation of this tool, nonprofit community-based social services professionals can cooperatively agree on work hours, safety mechanisms, etc. Some democratized nonprofits have teams who schedule workdays, coordinate salary increases, and stay attuned to community needs in flexible and lean ways. The power to make flexible and lean structural decisions can offset what many in nonprofit community-based social services organizations experience as being overwhelmed with over 40 hours per week workloads and no supports for curbing the negative impact of chronic stress and vicarious trauma.

How: Nonprofit Professional Employees Union (NPEU) can be your organization's partner for unionizing. Check them out at www.NPEU.org. Also, Sustainable Economies Law Center (SELC) trains nonprofits on how to transition into union-like models. Visit their website at www.theSELC. org to learn about their trainings and ongoing support.

Cost: Costs vary by training and support needs.

Tool 2: BIPOC Coaching

What: Outside coaches from Black, Indigenous, people of color (BIPOC) heritages can help your team by coaching small groups and/or one on one with team members. Hiring a coach to partner closely with small groups and/or individuals can support the articulation of two important things about organizational factors involved with unmitigated chronic stress and vicarious trauma. First, a BIPOC coach can help to identify culprits (i.e., routines, tasks, etc.) that small teams and/or individuals can address, keeping the coaching relationship and its benefits grounded among the employee base rather than the executive leadership. Second, a BIPOC coach can point out the fewest number of adjustments that have the greatest transformative effects for the team. Think of the widely known *80/20 rule* where 80 percent of any issue can be solved by addressing 20 percent of the factors involved (Burrell, 1985).

Why this tool is important: The BIPOC coach's presence inserted directly into the team, not reporting to the organizational leadership, can fuel a newly empowered team and/or individual action. Research studies across sectors show the powerful transformative impacts of BIPOC leaders, like consultant specialists, within white supremacy cultures for BIPOC staff and growth opportunities for white staff (Allen et al., 2021; Chaco, 2021; Chan et al., 2021). Studies can pinpoint the ways that BIPOC coaches can identify opportunities to address organizational values that may impede tool adoption. Hence, the importance of this tool is a double benefit. Also, depending on the history of your organization and culture, the coaching relationship can be safer for team members who rather not rock the boat openly. Confidentiality agreements could be used to ensure each individuals' privacy before, during, and after the coaching period.

How: Using an RFP process, seek BIPOC coaches who specialize in anti-racist and decolonizing practices in community facing organizations. An anti-racist and decolonizing lens can bring rich insights into your organization, identifying origin points for where unmitigated chronic stress and vicarious trauma is most robustly residing in practices, routines, and tasks. The RFP process should have the intention of finding BIPOC coaches who are hands-on with team empowerment and bring creative solutions for individuals and groups to utilize. Through the RFP process, your organization will learn from the conversations with several coach options, possibly expanding what your team initially imagined as the scope of coaching. There are great RFP templates and resources at www.techsoup.org.

Cost: Costs vary by depth and length of coaching, but estimate $250 an hour for a coach. Facilitation of the RFP process will cost staff time, including writing the RFP, spreading it through networks, and interviewing potential coaches.

Tool 3: Transparent Pay

What: Making salary structures known to all of the professionals on your organizational team supports greater connection because there are fewer secrets related to powerholding. For example, if the executive director makes four times the amount that direct service staff do, let's not hide that. Discussion of equitable treatment for talent should be had; remember that fear of conflict and emphasis on individualism are major features of white supremacy values. Your team might include team members from historically oppressed groups. If your organization's compensation model is reinforcing this oppression, this should be known and addressed collectively.

Why this tool is important: Research on salary transparency within organizations shows that transparency pay practices can reduce inequities and minimize previously existing pay gaps (Castilla, 2015). Research studies also show that when salaries are transparent to teams, sense of well-being can decrease or increase when the salary schedules appear equitable (Perez-Truglia, 2020). In addition to these benefits, power balance across the organization becomes increasingly possible because there are fewer secrets. As discussed elsewhere in this book, those with the most organizational discretionary power have the least direct exposure to job factors that create unmitigated vicarious trauma; and the inverse is also true. Shine light on the intersection of (a) job roles with high degrees of chronic stress and vicarious trauma and (b) pay equity. This can drive timely conversations about the health costs for nonprofit professionals whose career commitments are essential to the social services missions that are so vital to transforming social inequities.

How: There are three practices that are particularly useful for all sizes of nonprofits. Choose from any one, two, or all three practices: (1) Run a pay review to see where pay schedules are or are not equitable and which other compensation benefits are made available and used by the team (e.g., position titles, pay scales, raises, demographic indicators, years of experience, flextime, etc.). (2) Always post the pay range on job announcements and make sure that everyone who is already on the team with that same or similar role is being paid within the range. (3) Discuss and present information about pay equity with the current team and potential job candidates; define, reiterate, and share information about how your organization champions pay equity, supports a living wage, and how these align with the mission of your community-based social services organization.

Cost: There is no financial cost to using the three practices. However, there is staff time costs to consider, particularly for the first practice. Also, there are two free calculators of sorts: First, the U.S. Department of Labor has a cost-of-living calculator that is easy to use. Second, the National Conference on State Legislatures keeps track of state-by-state minimum wage laws. If there are pay inequities in your community-based organization, assume that your team already knows and that this is negatively impacting their trust in organizational leaders (Perez-Truglia, 2020).

Tool 4: CS & VT in Job Descriptions

What: Honestly indicate the job tasks that place the potential professional in the path of chronic stress and vicarious trauma. Professionals deserve to know this, particularly junior professionals new to community-based social services. Organizations need to reconsider what they ask of employees. Boards of Directors must see what the staff sacrifice to fulfill the organizational mission. Funders of the nonprofit sector need to see this *elephant in the room*.

Why this tool is important: Implementing a tool like this one cultivates trust among your team. Period. Research covered in this book shows the insidious ways that seemingly ordinary job activities create exposure points for nonprofit community-based social services professionals to experience chronic stress and vicarious trauma. New employees, new to nonprofit community-based social services or to the organization, can be ready and plan for how chronic stress and vicarious trauma will be part of the job experience. The only reason to not implement this tool is if the organizational leaders have no intention of implementing tools to mitigate the negative impact of chronic stress and vicarious trauma. It is unethical for organizations to withhold this information, creating situations where professionals wonder if they are losing their minds, don't have enough personal strength, and self-blaming for the ways that chronic stress and vicarious trauma are biologically taxing on them.

How: An ad hoc committee comprised of staff members from various parts of the organization can support the implementation of this tool. It is ideal to have direct service staff participate in the committee in order to think through the presence of hidden activities, practices, procedures, etc., that create chronic stress and vicarious trauma. Using the guide below and this book's chapter about the research on chronic stress and vicarious trauma will benefit the committee. Make sure that your organization's insurance carrier and/or labor attorney helps to inform the newly added wording to the job descriptions.

Cost: This tool is free because the guide below and this book's chapter on the research of chronic stress and vicarious trauma is accessible to readers.

CS and VT in Job Descriptions: A Guide

Description

This guide is intended to be used by an internal committee who is dedicated to making team members' exposure to chronic stress and vicarious trauma obvious within job description documents. In combination with the book *Nonprofit Work Is Killin' Me*, this guide supports the committee in identifying job tasks that carry the possibility of chronic stress and vicarious trauma so that new employees receive transparent explanations of the job responsibilities and expectations. The three activities should be engaged in the order presented.

Activities

- Review all organizational position titles in order to answer the following questions.
  - Which position titles refer to direct service roles?
  - Which position titles are not direct service roles but have customer service aspects with safety concerns for the employee?
  - Which of these titles require the employee to repeatedly engage persons who experience or are exposed to harm, safety issues, instability, etc.?
- Review one position description at a time in order to answer the following questions.
  - What are the essential functions of the job role that include the repeated use of skills like interviewing, completing assessments, engaging in self-defense, expressing compassion and empathy, etc.?

- ○ What percentage of the time are these skills being used in the position?
- Rewrite position descriptions that have any amount of engagement with community members who experience harm, safety issues, instability, etc.
  - ○ Indicate required job tasks that include chronic stress and vicarious trauma.
  - ○ Indicate required skills like interviewing, completing assessments, engaging in self-defense, expressing compassion and empathy, etc. that are to occur with community members who experience harm, safety issues, instability, etc.
  - ○ Somewhere in the job description, include a statement about the ways that your organization mitigates the negative impact of chronic stress and vicarious trauma.

Tool 5: Good Reason for Gatekeeping

What: The *Performance-Based Interview questions index* developed by the U.S. Veterans Administration (VA) is alarmingly precise. The interview questions were designed for providing interviewers with effective ways to garner the information needed for hiring the right team members. Refining your organizational structures and practices in order to mitigate chronic stress and vicarious trauma means that the organization must bring in team members, especially leadership, who support wellness, science, and innovation. Gatekeeping has historically been used to keep historically oppressed persons out of employment and leadership opportunities. However, with this tool, focus instead on welcoming in only those who share values that protect the team members who are experiencing the greatest blowback from chronic stress and vicarious trauma.

Why this tool is important: Studies show that hiring is one of the strongest opportunities to build an organizational culture and climate that is desired (Coe, Wiley, and Bekker, 2019). This tool borrows these facts and the practice of "gatekeeping" to make filtering who is and is not allowed into the organization. Across use, this tool can help your organization to hire professionals who champion team wellness, draw attention to organizational failures, and support the bigger commitment of mitigating chronic stress and vicarious trauma.

How: Review and assess the current state of the organization's interviewing process, including the existing interview questions, total number of questions, scoring rubric, and the calibration practices among interviewers in order to score job candidates in a uniform manner. Using the guide below called *Gatekeeping for Good Reason*, explore which of the listed wellness and innovation questions, from the *Performance-Based Interview questions index* developed by the VA, might be appropriate for your organization. Where wellness questions do not exist within the organization's interviewing template, add questions from the guide that align with the mission of your organization. Also, edit the scoring rubric to account for the addition of the new interview questions.

Cost: It is free to use the tool, but staff time for redesigning the hiring practices should be taken into consideration. Please see the free guide below.

Good Reason for Gatekeeping: A Guide

Description

These interview questions are slight adaptations of the *Performance-Based Interview questions index* developed by the U.S. Veterans Administration with modifications for nonprofit community-based social services organizations. Use these questions with your existing new hire protocol. This tool can help your organization to hire team members who champion staff wellness and innovation as well as support the bigger commitment of mitigating chronic stress and vicarious trauma.

Wellness Questions

Ask of...	Questions
Direct service roles	• Which of our wellness practices and supports attract you to our organization? • Describe a change in your approaches to working that you had to make in the last couple years. At the time, how did you feel about making the change? What did you do to make the change? How do you feel about the change now? • Describe a time when you anticipated potential problem(s) to your or your team's workload and developed ways to curb the problem(s). • Describe a situation where you felt you had not communicated well about your or your team's needs. How did you correct the situation?

Supervisory roles, in addition to all of the questions above	• Tell us about a time when you had to analyze staff performance appraisal information and make recommendations about coaching and mentoring team members. What kind of thought process did you go through? What was your reasoning behind your recommendations? • Tell me about a specific time you sought specific feedback on your performance from supervisees in terms of supporting their wellness and transparency. How did you use the feedback? Explain specific changes resulting from the feedback.
Executive roles, in addition to all of the questions above	• What are you doing to keep up with innovations in the management of teams in nonprofit community-based social services roles? What attributes do you possess that make you able to innovate? Explain specific examples. • Describe a time when you were faced with an obstacle to staff health and wellness? What did you do? Were you able to overcome the obstacle? What step(s) did you take?

Good Reasons for Gatekeeping (Side 2): A Guide

Innovation Questions

Ask of...	Questions
Direct service roles	• Tell me about two suggestions you have made to your supervisor in the past year. How did you come up with the ideas? What happened? How do you feel about the way things went? • Give examples to illustrate how you have generated ideas that represent thinking "outside the box" to benefit a team. How were your ideas received? What became of the ideas? • In your current job, what organizational change have you made or contributed to that you are proud of? How did you go about making the change? What has been the impact of the change?

Supervisory roles, in addition to all of the questions above	• Have you ever started a project on your own? Why did you start the project without a team? What were the results? • Explain the approach you use for innovating with programming. Explain specifically how you identify problems, what strategies you incorporate to determine the seriousness of the problems, how you come up with solutions that benefit the community and your team, and how you determine success and failure. Walk me through one problem you have dealt with from beginning to end. And what things would you do differently? • What things have you done to help your supervisees to better understand the relationship between their work and the work of (1) team members elsewhere in the organization as well as (2) organizations elsewhere in the community?
Executive roles, in addition to all of the questions above	• Describe a creative endeavor you led in the recent past that positively influenced the community who your current employer serves and the wellness of the organizational team. • Tell me about a specific time when you assisted your team in understanding the relevance of the organizational values in their job roles or projects. What modes did you use to communicate with them? How was the communication experienced by the team? How do you know this? • Tell me about a specific decision that you made within your organization that had unexpected consequences outside your organization as well as inside. How did you deal with those consequences? • According to Peter Senge, the one single thing a learning organization does well is to help people embrace change. Convince me that you are an effective change agent by describing an experience from your recent past where you helped change to be embraced by a team.

Tool 6: Offboard Mismatches

What: Saying goodbye to people who create fissures in the wellness and innovation values of the organization can be necessary for some organizations, be those people on the staff team or board of directors.

Similar to dissolving relationships with businesses or entries that are racist or homophobic, your organization has a duty to dissolve employment or membership on your team should they openly resist taking the needed steps to mitigate chronic stress and vicarious trauma.

Why this tool is important: The majority of team members who experience unmitigated chronic stress and vicarious trauma are female, BIPOC, and/or in the lowest paid job roles. These three historically oppressed groups have this experience because (1) women are the largest sex group in nonprofit community-based social services organizations, (2) BIPOC professionals most readily access entry-level, direct service jobs, and (3) direct service jobs are the lowest paid positions. Hence, when a team or Board member disregards your organization's investments in team wellness, this person is consciously or unconsciously saying much more than they just don't like wellness investments. The person is also saying that professionals from historically oppressed backgrounds are not worthy of supports to mitigate chronic stress and vicarious trauma.

How: Ensure that all legally required actions are addressed before offboarding the person. Then, using the steps below, exit the person with the intention of wishing them success elsewhere. The steps can support your organization in a smooth transition during such an offboarding. The difficulty that can exist with offboarding primarily falls within the context of Human Resources and accountability structures such as adherence to regular performance appraisals. Without these structures, team members who are mismatches for the wellness and innovation values of the organization might stay too long and injure the team.

Cost: A free guide to assist your organization is below, but the existing costs for the organization's insurance policy and labor lawyer must factor into the costs for this tool.

Offboard Mismatches: A Guide

Description

When a team or Board member opposes your organization's investments in team wellness, this person is consciously or unconsciously saying much more than they just don't like wellness investments. They are also saying that team members from historically oppressed backgrounds are not worthy of supports to mitigate chronic stress and vicarious trauma. The steps below help your organization to exit the person with the intention of wishing them success elsewhere.

Steps

- Ensure that all legally required measures are addressed before offboarding the person.
- Tangible evidence should exist with the appropriate Human Resources structures such as performance appraisal notes, signatures, emails, etc.
- When possible, the person receives ample time to search for a new position such as 4- to 6-weeks.
- Where the offboarding person has strengths, support the person with letters of recommendations and emails of introduction to enhance their job search, but include the persons failures surrounding team wellness. Future employers should know about the person's strengths and areas for concern.
- A few days in advance of the person's final day, announce the person's departure in a manner that the person deems appropriate.
- Curb any potential fear that may be leaking from friendships among the team around the departure of a team member. For example, ask for those concerns to be submitted through an anonymous survey or other private methods that can buffer real or perceived concerns about the person's offboarding. Organizational leadership must respond to each voiced fear verbally and in a timely manner. Transparency is vital for teams while also considering the person's privacy.

Reflections

_____

_____

_____

_____

_____

Tool 7: Retreats Are Not Treats

What: Learning, skill-building, and strengthening connections among team members is vital for organizations. This is especially the case for organizations that are undertaking adjustments to their structures and practices entangled in team suffering. The learning, skill-building, and connecting can unfold as an organizational retreat with the guide presented below. Importantly, retreats are not *indulgences* bestowed by executive leadership. Retreats are central parts of a strategically led organization.

Why this tool is important: Research studies show that team retreats can supply the participants with targeted empowerment to advance specific skills and also to act as transformational momentum (Guastello and Frampton, 2014). By implementing a tool like this one, a team retreat focused on studying and planning for mitigating chronic stress and vicarious trauma can transform the team by exposing them to new scientific knowledge, creative tools, and informing strategy sessions on how to address systemic issues within the organization.

How: A retreat that births and/or unveils innovations for mitigating chronic stress and vicarious trauma will empower the nonprofit community-based social services professionals who make the magic happen. Using the tool below, make sure that the retreat has learning features for the team and includes a method for understanding what the team is learning and walking away with from the retreat so that your organization knows whether or not the retreat fulfilled its purpose. Consider hosting at a retreat space surrounded by positive visual stimulation (i.e., the positive impact of green scenery was discussed earlier in the book) and opportunities for walks and movement (i.e., walking activities were discussed earlier in the book).

Cost: Rental space fees that may or may not include meals rage up to $1,000 per day for a small team. Consider collaborating with another nonprofit community-based social services organization to have a shared retreat in order to share the costs and gain collective insights across your organizations (Bartczak, 2015). A retreat facilitator can cost another $1,000 per day; use the RFP process described above for the coaching tool to find a BIPOC consulting specialist. Pre-retreat planning activities are free of cost with the following guide.

Retreats Are Not Treats: A Guide

Description

Research studies show that team retreats can supply the participants with targeted empowerment to advance specific skills and also to act as transformational momentum. With the steps below, plan to expose the team to new scientific knowledge, creative tools, and informing strategy sessions on how to address systemic issues within the organization. This guide is intended to be used by the ad hoc committee who is in charge of mapping out the retreat design.

Steps For Planning

- **Establish the scope of the retreat.** Develop the retreat design on the why, how, and when of each activity that comprises the retreat agenda.
- **Schedule the retreat.** Email a "save the date" to all team members (and/or volunteers) with instructions to schedule the event as part of paid time.
- **Facilitate an RFP process.** Identify the best BIPOC retreat facilitator(s) for addressing chronic stress and vicarious trauma. Refer to tools in this chapter for tips on facilitating an RFP process.
- **Build the retreat agenda with the retreat facilitator's deliverables. Deliverables might be worded in the following ways.**
  - The team gains knowledge and skills that support them with implementing tools that mitigate chronic stress and vicarious trauma.
  - The team contributes to refining organizational practices that can mitigate chronic stress and vicarious trauma.
  - The team cultivates interpersonal opportunities to discuss the organization's cultural values, official and implicit values.
  - The team applies strategic decision-making that can inform organizational structures and practices.
  - The executive leadership commit to fulfilling the plans developed at the retreat within the next four seasons.

- **Other planning.** Schedule supplies, meals, transportation, etc. Finalize retreat agenda and curriculums for sending to the team in advance of go-day.

Steps for Understanding What the Team Walked Away With

- **Seek understanding.** Follow up immediately after the retreat with an impressions survey in order to gather team feedback on the benefits and/or gains made to their knowledge, skills, and connections.
- **Seek insights on learning.** In terms of seeking understanding about gains made with knowledge and skills, prompts could include the following.
  - I gained knowledge on what chronic stress and vicarious trauma are. Response options: I learned a lot; I learned just enough; I barely learned anything new; I learned nothing.
  - I gained knowledge on how to mitigate chronic stress and vicarious trauma. Response options: Same as above.
  - I gained skills on how I can individually mitigate chronic stress and vicarious trauma. Response options: Same as above.
  - I gained skills on how my team can mitigate chronic stress and vicarious trauma. Response options: Same as above.
- **Seek insights on connectedness:** In terms of seeking understanding about gains made around team connectedness, prompts could include the following.
  - I directly helped to develop at least one new or revised practice. Response options: Fully agree; partially agree/disagree; fully disagree.
  - My teammates shared speaking time, allowing me to participate as much as I felt necessary. Response options: Same as above.
  - I increased my trust or confirmed my trust is well-placed with one or more team members. Response options: Same as above.
  - I increased my trust or confirmed my trust is well-placed with one or more supervisors. Response options: Same as above.

- **Plan the next retreat.** Share the results from the impressions survey with the team. This can be a central feature in planning the next staff retreat and even inform designing activities for the next retreat agenda.

Tool 8: Join a Study

What: Partnering with universities and research centers can position your organization for free support. Many scientists are already developing tools that mitigate chronic stress and vicarious trauma in various job sectors. Find an opportunity to offer your team as a study participant.

Why this tool is important: Many nonprofit community-based social services organizations are fascinating spaces of community transformation and complex spaces of team injury and healing. Also, many of these organizations have lean budgets and infrastructures, collaborating with a researcher and scientist could be a perfect match for your organization. Researchers and scientists love collaborating with organizations that are already innovative but that do not have the funds to bring in the range of tools needed to mitigate chronic stress and vicarious trauma.

How: Using the guide below, select any or all of the actions listed. The focus with this tool is finding potential partnerships with researchers and scientists who will add value to your organization's investment in mitigating the negative impact of chronic stress and vicarious trauma.

Cost: The guide below makes this tool free, except for staff time to implement it.

Join a Study: A Guide

Description

Position your organization for free support by partnering with universities and research centers who specialize in mitigating chronic stress and vicarious trauma. Many nonprofit community-based social services organizations are fascinating spaces of community transformation and complex spaces of team injury and healing. The activities in this guide allow you to provide researchers with the gift of getting to know and serve your team.

Activities

- Put out a position description that indicates your organization is interested in serving as a research subject for researchers. Also list your organizational mission; some notes about the chronic stress and vicarious trauma that are part of the social services roles; and the temperament and skills needed for a partnership. Spread the position description throughout your professional network and definitely academic listservs.
- Make calls and schedule face-to-face exchanges with many researchers in your professional network. During these exchanges, share content like that put into the position description described above. After the face-to-face exchanges, be sure to follow up with a gift of thanks to those who made time to speak with you and discuss your team's needs.
- Ask trusted persons in your professional network to send the position description, discussed above, further into their own professional networks.
- Once you identify one or more potential partnerships, seek feedback from your elders about the potential partnership. Having seen many types of collaborations in their lives, elders have important wisdom to guide you and your team.
- Once you have an agreed upon partnership with researchers, make sure that there is a Memorandum of Understanding (MOU) that outlines the scope and requirements of the partnership. Also ensure that all on your staff team sign confidentiality agreements, as appropriate.

Reflections

_____
_____
_____
_____
_____

Tool 9: HR Practices Focused on CS & VT

What: Adding seven seemingly small Human Resources (HR) practices to your organization's infrastructure can interrupt existing cultural inclinations to work nonstop, overlook staff suffering, and even ignore safety issues faced by your team members due to the dynamics of carrying out social services job roles central to your organization's mission. In the guide below, identify which of the seven HR practices can be cultivated into the soil of your organization.

Why this tool is important: Let's be real. Many, many, many nonprofit community-based organizations do not have budgets that allow for HR managers. Who is handling HR? Anyone's guess is a good one! Sometimes the executive director manages many HR responsibilities and then outsourced other HR tasks to third party agencies. The guide below has practical, easy to implement HR practices for the majority of organizations out there. That is, many such organizations are scrappy, smart, and on the move. HR infrastructure is frequently overlooked.

How: Use the guide below to identify all that is missing and make notes about the practical reality of how quickly each of the practices can be integrated into the rhythms of your organization.

Cost: The guide below makes this tool free, but staff time is needed for implementation.

HR Practices Focused on CS & VT: A Guide

Description

The actions encouraged in this guide are sensible, easy to implement HR practices for the majority of organizations out there. Many such organizations are scrappy, smart, and on the move. HR practices can help to mitigate the negative impact of chronic stress and vicarious trauma experienced by team members with direct service job roles.

Practices

- **Performance appraisals.** Add a dimension to your organization's performance appraisal process. When drafting appraisals, all team members can write about their experiences with implementing tools for mitigating chronic stress and vicarious trauma, both at the level of their job roles and their department or unit.

- **Supervision meetings.** During regularly held one-on-one supervision and coaching meetings, team members and their supervisors should use a discussion sheet to remember to discuss recent events and/or issues pertaining to chronic stress and vicarious trauma during job tasks.
- **Wellness resources.** Revise the health and operational insurance plans to increase wellness resource bundles available to the team that can help to mitigate chronic stress and vicarious trauma at the individual and organizational levels. Remember, workplace suffering is not an individual's problem nor can this be solved at the individual level.
- **Compensation alternatives.** Create meaningful alternatives to salary increases such as work from home days, bring the child or dog to work plans, priority parking spots, monthly gift certificates, discounts at gyms or with private Personal Trainers, etc. Research studies discussed elsewhere in this book show that pay is typically the third reason that nonprofit employees resign from their organization.
- **Boundaries when on leave.** Require away messages to be automatically programmed into emails in order to ensure boundaries exist between worktime and leave. Have the messages read something like this: "To address your email or need, please email the following person: _____. I am away until [insert date] and our organizational policy does not allow me to invest time in addressing emails that come in while I am on leave. Please know that we care about your email so please email the address above or re-email me upon my return."
- **Promote mental health.** Require all organizational leaders to attend at least six sessions of counseling in order to diminish the stigma around caring for mental health. Leaders can even bring their counselors to lecture about what counseling is with the team during in-house training days.

- **Ensure safety.** Revise organizational policies to ensure that safety at the offices and around the premises is ensured. When team members work late hours or are alone in the offices, they should be ensured that the organization is looking out for them. For example, door locks and alarm systems should be checked on a reoccurring schedule for maintenance purposes. No one on your team should have to negotiate with an unknown man who entered the building from an accidentally unlocked fence, only to leave after he exposes his genitalia and screams profanity. True story. Also, earlier in this book, we met nonprofit professionals placed in neighborhoods with safety issues. Policies must be updated to address such issues.

Reflections

_____

_____

_____

_____

Tool 10: Supervisory
and Coaching Meetings

What: Research studies about employment and management sciences show that there are three top reasons for job burnout, unfolding in this order: Workload, personnel issues, and compensation. Workload!!! Brain studies show that for every hour of work after 50 hours, the effectiveness of that work significantly decreases. The guide below supports supervisors in their role to support employees with workload, investing attention at the intersection of workload, personnel issues, chronic stress and vicarious trauma.

Why: Studies show that help with workload and personnel issues can be deeply meaningful to your team. Further, cross-cultural employment research shows that even high performing countries with Western cultural practices similar to those of the U.S. (e.g., Germany) remain extremely productive even when the workday ends after eight hours. Supervisors have the responsibility, whether or not they know this, to advocate for their team members; this includes buffering the nonprofit cultural fixation with urgency and individualism. Team members experience increased levels of job satisfaction, satisfaction with their teams and job responsibilities, when they are heard by leadership and peers, their job goals are coherent, and they have a clear path for contributing to the well-being of the collective team. Ultimately, this tool is not about the individual.

How: Supervisory and coaching meetings must be weekly or bimonthly in order to create a rhythm of support. Detrimental aspects among the team can be identified more quickly with regularly occurring meetings such as job tasks, routines, and protocols that create exposure to chronic stress and vicarious trauma. Also, the guide below assumes that supervisors are appropriately skilled for supporting their team members.

Cost: There is free access to the guide below, but expanding your supervisors' skills for implementing the activities in the guide might require your organizational budget to include the need for supervisor training opportunities.

Supervisory and Coaching Meetings: A Guide

Description

In this order, workload, personnel issues, and compensation are linked to employees resigning from their organizations. Team members experience increased levels of job satisfaction when they are heard by leadership and peers, their job goals are coherent, and they have a clear path for contributing to the well-being of the collective team. The activities below are for supervisors to implement on a reoccurring basis during their one-to-one time with team members.

Supervisor Activities

- **Overtime.** Is the staff member working over 40 hours per week or beyond their pay plan? Decide what actions the organization can take to stop or reduce this. Ensure that this is not a conversation about *efficiency*, rather an exploration of the reality of what it takes to accomplish jobs tasks, officially or unofficially, piled on top of the team member.
- **Exposure.** How often does the team member experience direct interactions with community members (e.g., program participants, trainees, clients, etc.) that create chronic stress

152

and vicarious trauma? Refer to the chapter in this book that focuses on the science of chronic stress and vicarious trauma.

- **Tools.** What individual and organization level tools exist in your organization to help mitigate chronic stress and vicarious trauma? Is the staff member using those? Explore dynamics in the team that may or may not support the implementation of these tools.

- **White supremacy.** Does the team member subscribe to white supremacy values discussed earlier in this book? For example, does the team member brag about the small amount of sleep that they get, frequent illnesses, hustling, not taking a lunch break, etc.? Explore what training might be needed for your team surrounding the damage caused to the team by intentionally or unintentionally championing white supremacy values in the workplace. When considering possible training options, return to the chapter on nonprofit sector culture and norms.

- **Attendance.** Does the team member attend all supervisory meetings with you? If not, why is this occurring? Examine features in your relationship with the team member that may incubate subtle conflict and have an open conversation with the team member.

- **Special needs.** For topics that the team member doesn't want to share with you such as safety issues, team dynamics, etc., is the team member familiar with the processes for seeking help elsewhere? Ensure that team members know that while you are their first resource, you can bridge the team member to another supervisor temporarily if there is a special need that you cannot resolve.

Tool 11: Alter Strategic Planning

What: Strategic planning practices can mitigate chronic stress and vicarious trauma. The tool below includes strategic planning activities that can guide your organization's investments in ways that encourage team wellness and ensure the voices from the team inform the strategic plan. Those on the team who have job roles with minimal discretionary power are important informers of the organizations next few years of planning. Ultimately, direct service staff are those who are most often exposed to chronic stress and vicarious trauma and can provide important insights for organizational strategies that inform contributions to the community, collaboration with partner agencies, and relationships with funders.

Why this tool is important: Altering the ways that organizational priorities and strategies are put together can impact the structures and practices that either resolve or further embed unmitigated chronic stress and vicarious trauma among your team. For example, when building a strategic plan, organizations must consider the social problem(s) that their mission is designed to heal. This problem is identified in order to inspire succinct solutions and arguments for those solutions. Many of these strategic planning solutions rely on well planned program designs as well as careful resource allocation; the very activities involved in fulfilling the organizational mission distill into activities for program implementation which bridges program staff to contexts rife with chronic stress and traumatized populations. Also, resource allocation frequently excludes comprehensive attention to mitigating the negative impact of chronic stress and vicarious trauma that is essentially required to fulfilling the organizational mission.

How: Implementing a tool like the one below can help your organization to link the design of organizational strategies to innovative solutions to mitigate exposure to chronic stress and vicarious trauma. Researchers on organizational design in service contexts remind us that "less efficient [organizational] designs drain precious resources and hamper efforts to deliver the best care possible" (Elrod and Fortenberry, 2017: 25). This includes organizational designs that ignore and/or normalize unmitigated suffering of the team who are the foundation of the organizational mission.

Cost: The inclusion of strategic planning practices that focus attention on team wellness, as well as ensure team ownership over the strategic plan, can have zero new costs. A free guide is below and is for use with whomever your organization plans to partner with for strategic planning (i.e., a strategic planning consultant). Strategic planning typically costs tens of thousands of dollars depending on the size of the organization, though this is planned for in the budgets of organizations. We recommend partnering with a BIPOC consultant team through an RFP process, as discussed earlier in this chapter.

Alter Strategic Planning: A Guide

Description

This guide supports nonprofit community-based organizations with altering how they typically engage in strategic planning. It is vital that organizations comprehensively include strategies that mitigate chronic stress and vicarious trauma, curbing the suffering of what staff are tasked with doing to fulfill the organizational mission. The two sections of the guide can be engaged in any order.

Wellness Priorities

- In the previous Strategic Plan document, identify which priorities unintentionally fueled chronic stress and vicarious trauma among the team. Use the chapter in this book about the research that explains chronic stress and vicarious trauma.
- Train the entire team, including the executive leaders and Board, about the negative impact of unmitigated chronic stress and vicarious trauma. Facts must drive strategic planning.
- Identify science-backed wellness supports that already exist in the organization. Assess whether they are are mitigating the negative impact of chronic stress and vicarious trauma.
- Discuss the organizational data on the use trends for sick time, vacation, and staff retention. Use the data to inform team wellness strategies.

Staff Ownership Priorities

- Assess your team's current exposure to and understanding of the Strategic Plan. For example, ask for anonymous survey responses with prompts like the following:
  - My choices and opinions were valued in the process of creating the Strategic Plan. Response options: Agree, Sometimes Agree, Disagree, I did not participate in the development of the Strategic Plan.
  - I know how my job role fulfills parts of the Strategic Plan, directly and indirectly. Response options: Agree, Sometimes Agree, Disagree.
  - I can look to my supervisor for guidance on how our

organization is addressing chronic stress and vicarious trauma that stems from our social services work. Response options: Agree, Sometimes Agree, Disagree.
• Design strategic planning practices that involved and are even led by staff across all parts of your organization.

Reflections

_____

_____

_____

_____

Closing

The 11 organizational tools described in this chapter can help you to lead your team in mitigating the negative impact of chronic stress and vicarious trauma. Along with the two approaches for priming your organization for meaningful tool adoption, you can help to amplify the capacities across your entire team to collectively transform the ways that your team does their mission-driven jobs.

A spirit of experimentation is powerful, but so too is knowing that your team's exposure to chronic stress and vicarious trauma is not individually created nor individually solved. This chapter is about taking responsibility for organizations and any of its failures to understand and address the links between team suffering and racism and classism. There are push and pull forces inside and outside of nonprofit community-based organizations. These forces are intentionally stifling to the missions of community-based organizations that are focused on transforming social inequities. Use the tools in this chapter to support how you walk through your leadership identity knowing that you are doing your best and your best now must include understanding the organizational responsibility to prioritize team wellness.

11 Organization Level Tools

Which tools will we experiment with?

_____

☐ Tool 1: *Unionize Your Nonprofit*
☐ Tool 2: *BIPOC Coaching*

☐ Tool 3: *Transparent Pay*
☐ Tool 4: *CS & VT in Job Descriptions*
☐ Tool 5: *Good Reasons for Gatekeeping*
☐ Tool 6: *Offboard Mismatches*
☐ Tool 7: *Retreats Are Not Treats*
☐ Tool 8: *Join a Study*
☐ Tool 9: *HR Practices Focused on CS & VT*
☐ Tool 10: *Supervisory and Coaching Meetings*
☐ Tool 11: *Alter Strategic Planning*

Reflections

_____

_____

_____

_____

CHAPTER 6

Sector Level Tools

The focus of this final chapter dedicated to tools supports readers with developing and implementing solutions for mitigating chronic stress and vicarious trauma in nonprofit community-based social services organizations by targeting the sector culture and norms. To recall the workings of the nonprofit sector culture and norms, refer to the earlier chapter that focuses on just this topic. The conditions for unmitigated chronic stress and vicarious trauma throughout thousands of nonprofit community-based social services organizations relies on a collective agreement that ongoing suffering for women, BIPOC persons, and low paid team members are just fine.

While a lot can be accomplished at the individual and organizational levels, as illustrated in the earlier chapters with tools relevant to those levels, shifting the nonprofit sector culture and norms by shifting whose voice gets heard and what gets advocated for is also part of the process of halting the slow *killin'* off of nonprofit community-based social services professionals. The nonprofit sector culture and norms reflect the greater U.S. cultural context of racism and classism. The details about the link between nonprofit sector culture and norms and racism and classism is fully explained for readers in an earlier chapter. Further, the link between unmitigated chronic stress and vicarious trauma and racism and classism is fully explained as well. However, let's briefly recall that the sector culture reinforces racist and classist norms, orbiting religiously to the following:

- Good people are willing to sacrifice in the course of service.
- Caring for other people is the focus of charitable activities.
- If there was a problem, then leadership would solve it.

Within these three norms, and hidden for some readers, are the following racist and classist commitments:

- *Good people are willing to sacrifice in the course of service* is essentially a classist cultural belief, where working laborers into exhaustion is normalized.

- *Caring for other people is the focus of charitable activities* is at the core a racist cultural belief. This norm focuses the nonprofit organization's response to social inequities, social inequities created from racism, as simply about "caring enough" rather than focusing on adjusting the human value hierarchy and the ways it is used to distribute social, economic, and political power in the community and inside of the organization.
- *If there was a problem, then leadership would solve it* is also at the core a classist cultural belief. This norm reinforces the power relationship between workers and their managers, where workers hold and/or access less social, economic, and political power to address the tangible needs surrounding unmitigated chronic stress and vicarious trauma.

Earlier in this book, we explored the research studies, including one conducted by me through my faculty role at California State University, Fresno. Refer back to that chapter to see all of the data. Here, let us briefly recall that among nonprofit community-based social services teams, 15 percent to 72 percent are experiencing chronic stress. This range represents 11 indicators of chronic stress developed by medical researchers (Aparicio et al., 2013; Kristensen et al., 2005). For example, 72 percent confirm they do not have *enough energy for family and friends during leisure time.* Among these professionals, 61 percent of them were working more than 40 hours per week in their roles to transform the lives of community members. Further, 13 percent to 24 percent show that they are experiencing vicarious trauma. For example, 24 percent find themselves *thinking about distressing client/program participant issues outside of work* and sometimes feeling *helpless to assist clients in the way I would like.*

What will the other side of implemented solutions look like? The tools in this chapter can be engaged by anyone in any role in a community-based social services organization. You do not have to be in an executive leadership role to engage the tools here. As with the earlier chapters focused on tools, the focus on sector wide tools is outlined with the following features for each: *what, why, how,* and *cost.* Everyone can contribute to altering the nonprofit sector culture and norms.

Tool Curation Methods

The tools in this chapter were curated for nonprofit professionals in social services organizations with several things in mind. First, the tools were selected so that you can implement them no matter your job role because the tools impact factors outside of your responsibilities to your organization. Attention to team wellness in the nonprofit sector is treated like a recreational pastime, if at all. Team wellness must be understood as ensuring mission impact and countering racism and classism. Second, all of the tools in this chapter are free outside of the time it takes you to implement them. Third, the tools reflect research studies that can inspire confidence in our use of them. Nonprofit folks love data and facts for guiding us to what makes a sustainable change in our communities. Fourth, the tools are not designed for individual use, rather, please use these collectively with colleagues and friends.

Unmitigated chronic stress and vicarious trauma is *harm*. We explored the research behind this fact in medical and management sciences. Mitigating chronic stress and vicarious trauma refers to *reducing* the intensity, lengthiness, and fallout of it; chronic stress and vicarious trauma is expected to be a part of nonprofit community-based social services work, but unmitigated dynamics do not need to be. Readers must not wait for the nonprofit sector to culturally shift its norms discussed earlier in this book; major cultural shifts do not occur without action. Ultimately, the curation of the tools was done for you, the reader, with care about the longevity of your career in nonprofit community-based social services organizations and with appreciation for investing your energy in transforming social inequities.

Engaging the Tools

There are four things to do in order to get ready for implementing the tools below. The four approaches to priming yourself for using the tools will help you to grow your capacity for making careful brush strokes when instigating change; having a good time doing it; and cultivating allies. First, join existing committees and groups within nonprofit entities. Select carefully where you spend your time and attention, identifying possible enriching relationships with those who focus on the broad topic of *mission impact*. Here are a few options:

- The National Council of Nonprofits (NCN) and the 41 state level chapters have specified project priorities. In California, their chapter has an annual convention, perfect for elevating the issues surrounding unmitigated chronic stress and vicarious trauma. In Michigan, their chapter has the Capacity Building

Center Network (CBCN) that serves Michigan nonprofit needs around strengthening the organizational infrastructure and impact. Because many social services teams are suffering from unmitigated chronic stress and vicarious trauma, the CBCN is an ideal group with which to collaborate. Each of the 41 state chapters has opportunities like these two examples, allowing you opportunities to expand your allies and to become an ally to many.

- BoardSource focuses on cultivating coherent Board leadership teams. While BoardSource does not yet have a priority area reflective of the discussion in this book on unmitigated chronic stress and vicarious trauma, they have a lengthy consultant index. Again, the index does not allow readers to see which consultants focus on deconstructing nonprofit sector culture and norms that are the underpinning source of unmitigated chronic stress and vicarious trauma. However, those consultants with expertise in the two areas of inclusion and mission impact can serve as future allies. Engage them and support them. BoardSource is the major outlet for nonprofit Board training in the U.S.
- The University of Southern California Price School of Public Policy has an array for departments and units, including a master's degree program in nonprofit management. The program encompasses faculty and nonprofit leaders who focus on social impact and nonprofit infrastructure design, two areas relevant to *mission impact*. These two areas must also contend with unmitigated chronic stress and vicarious trauma and, hence, can be a great outlet for developing allies and with whom, once relationships bloom, to implement the tools below.

Based on your life circumstances, select associations that are local, regional, state, and national. And, most importantly for priming yourself for using the tools below, be the voice for educating your budding allies about the links among:

- unmitigated chronic stress and vicarious trauma;
- racism and classism in the nonprofit sector and the U.S. more widely; and
- what counts as demonstrations of mission impact.

Second, if a local nonprofit management focused coalition does not exist, then create one with a charter about the linkages listed above. It is important for many of our lifestyles and passions that we can collaborate locally. If such a coalition already exists, become a committed and regularly attending member of the coalition. The membership and its contributions to nonprofits locally must include education and actions surrounding how to mitigate chronic stress and vicarious trauma among the social services organization that comprise some segment of the coalition.

Third, ask for permission to participate in ongoing learning from existing anti-racist organizations, groups, and activities that are focused on transforming oppressions and biases in various ways. These entities do not need to be focused on the same topic matter that you are a specialist on (i.e., teen parenting programs). Focusing on learning about and how to uproot racism and classism in any topic matter will increase your capacity to articulate information about racism and classism, help you to understand the research on the intersection of oppression and chronic stress and vicarious trauma, and grow a family of allies. For example, here are a few such anti-racist organizations:

- Naya Family Center in Portland, Oregon, is a major regional influencer, demonstrating how to grow knowledge, skills, and comfort with returning to indigenous food ways. Their calendar of events is open to the community, indigenous to the area or not. If you were to want to learn from the Center, explore what you can from their online activities and resources surrounding how they are transforming oppressions and biases in relation to food, food access, and food's impact on the longevity of the people. Where appropriate, be sure to pay for content when that is requested. After you have spent time learning about the wisdom of how the Center is transforming oppressions and biases, incorporate the insights that you learned into your use of the nonprofit sector levels tools in this chapter.
- The National Center on Violence Against Women in the Black Community, also known as Ujima, in Washington, D.C. is an expert team providing education and consulting on domestic and sexual violence. Their resources can help you to learn about the systemic oppressions and biases at the interpersonal, community, and societal levels surrounding how Black women experience such violence. When you watch their online webinars and listen to the Ujima podcast, observe the ways that interpersonal, community, and societal oppressions show up for Black women inside and outside the scope of different forms of violence. As a rigorous organization, we can gain immensely from the wisdom that this team gives to the country.

- Salud America! in Texas is an educational organization that focuses on research and advocacy around improving policies and systems for the health of Latinx families and children. Their educational content is available online. They provide you with an opportunity to see how research and advocacy by a BIPOC organization is increasing attention to oppressions and biases surrounding health across the country. Like above, explore what you can from their online resources and, where appropriate, be sure to pay for content when that is requested. After you have spent time learning about the wisdom of how their team is drawing attention to oppressions and biases experienced by Latinx families and children, incorporate these insights into your use of the nonprofit sector level tools in this chapter.

These entities have a wealth of wisdom that can amplify your skills and commitment to mitigating chronic stress and vicarious trauma. Remember to show gratitude to the anti-racist organizations that you learn from whether you are white or BIPOC; that is, there are many BIPOC persons who are acculturated to white supremacy values, enacting the same colonizing behavior as whites are often programmed into. For example, avoid colonizing etiquette like don't reach out to these organizations for free advising. When in conversation with anti-racist organization, avoid correcting our speech, interrupting with your exciting ideas, and assume that we know more about those with white heritage than you know about us. These are reflective of the dominant cultural beliefs and practices in this country. With my fair skin and Ivy League training, I have had to counter white acculturation programming frequently, disentangling myself from the pull and grip of white supremacy values. Many of us light skinned BIPOC persons are vulnerable to reinforcing oppressive values and behavior. Don't do that. Nobody needs you to bring this into their work life. In fact, conduct an internet search or read books like *Nice Racism* by DiAngelo (2021), discussed in earlier chapters, to help you to exhibit all of the beautiful humility with which you can walk the earth.

Finally, if you are an executive level leader, ensure that your Board of Directors team is fully committed to mitigating chronic stress and vicarious trauma. If you are not an executive level leader, propose this approach to your executive leaders and to associations and consultants who train Board members. Educate them; provide them with doorways to walk through for demonstrating their commitment such as with the tools below; and, hopefully, future Board members will be recruited with a commitment to mitigating chronic stress and vicarious trauma in order to accomplish mission impact and, dang, how about just do the most legit thing possible to support transformation inside and outside of nonprofit community-based social services organizations.

Tools

Tool 1: Write Intentional Letters

What: Writing letters to funders, nonprofit college degree programs, and professional associations can impact nonprofit sector practices. In your letters, tell the recipients that enough is enough. Share this book, the data, and your vision for a different way for nonprofit community-based social services organizational teams to fulfill their organizational missions.

Why this tool is important: Research studies show us that those in power positions need to hear directly from you about the issues that you know need to be resolved with their support. For example, studies on the responses of politicians in western countries shows that members of legislatures are likely to implement your call to action if you directly contact them and as long as you are a resident of their district or zone (Naurin and Ohberg, 2013). This translates as reaching out directly to local, regional, and state nonprofit leadership. Sharing the facts about the widespread problem of unmitigated chronic stress and vicarious trauma will be shocking to some. Sharing about the three linkages above might also shock some. This information has not been widely explained in the sector, hence the writing of this book.

How: Below is a straightforward template. In your letter, handwritten or typed, make sure that data points about the widespread experiences with chronic stress and vicarious trauma are centrally displayed. This topic should not be disputed and data often helps readers who may be quick to dismiss unless the data is immediately in front of them. You will see more components in the template below. If you feel it is best, write the letter anonymously and explain why you are sending the letter anonymously; the recipient must come to understand the true threat that some of us face in terms of job security. Write to funders, nonprofit associations, social entrepreneurship centers, and government agencies who interact with nonprofits, whoever you think may want to help alter the nonprofit sector culture and norms. Set up a reminder in your calendar to write and send letters on a regular basis.

Cost: The template is free. Asking a friend or new ally to review and edit your letter is also free.

[Write Date]

[Write Recipient Name]
[Write Recipient Title]
[Write Recipient's Organization Name]
[Write Recipient Address]
[Write Recipient Address]

Dear [Write Recipient Name],

Nonprofit community-based social services organizations are known for their effective responses to major threats in the community as well as leading systemic transformations to resolve social issues. Many of the staff teams who comprise these organizations are significantly suffering from widespread unmitigated chronic stress and vicarious trauma. For example:

- [Write the data points that you are most drawn to share.]
- [Write the data points that you are most drawn to share.]
- [Write the data points that you are most drawn to share.]

[Write one to two sentences about why you are reaching out to this person specifically. What role does this person have and/or what has this person said or written about recently that is tied to chronic stress and vicarious trauma in nonprofit community-based social services organizations?]

[Write two to three sentences about your job role in a social services organization. How long you have been working in this sector and what are your passions to serve in this way?]

[In two to three sentences, write your direct observations and/or experiences with unmitigated chronic stress and vicarious trauma. This is an opportunity to paint a picture for the recipient.]

[Write your call to action, stating what the recipient can contribute in order to solve the problem. Do you want to speak with this person directly to brainstorm next steps? Do you want a specific resource required for all nonprofit community-based social services organizations in your state? Do you want mandated education on racism within the nonprofit sector for members of a certain association?]

165

[Write one to two sentences thanking the recipient for their time.]

Sincerely,

[Write Your Name]

[Sign Your Name]

[Write Your Contact Information]

Tool 2: Speak Widely

What: Speak about the data and experiences of unmitigated chronic stress and vicarious trauma at as many events as you can. Whenever a local, regional, state, or national opportunity opens, take it. Also speak about the resources that are accessible to all of us, experiences of you and your nonprofit colleagues, and the importance of understanding the linkages of three intersecting issues discussed earlier in this book:

- unmitigated chronic stress and vicarious trauma;
- racism and classism in the nonprofit sector and the U.S. more widely; and
- what counts as demonstrations of mission impact

Why this tool is important: Research studies show us that people accept a standard and agree that it is important when they are tasked with generating arguments for it (Lemmen et al., 2020). Further, engaging groups in developing arguments and counterarguments for a specific solution can potentially strengthen the validity of the solution (Jonassen and Kim, 2010). Hence, implementing this tool is a great opportunity to weave in research on persuading the adoption of standards and solutions into your opportunities to speak widely about unmitigated chronic stress and vicarious trauma.

How: There are annual conferences and events as well as speaking opportunities at universities and meet-up groups in your region, state, and nationally. It does not matter what your job role is; you do not need permission from anyone to speak about this topic as long as you don't name anyone or any organization without their permission. You have permission to borrow information from this book, but please cite as appropriate. I am not trying to get rich here; this book is a gift to those I love so very much in the nonprofit sector. Ultimately, there is no approval process for gathering with allies and educating the masses. Conduct an internet search with search terms like the following. These can help you to identify opportunities to formally submit speaking proposals as workshop topics, panel events, and so forth.

- "Nonprofit conference"
- "Annual conference [write name of city or state]"
- "Nonprofit workshop"
- "Nonprofit panel"
- "Nonprofit training"

Most speaking opportunities will have an online form to complete where you will see requirements like a 250 word abstract, "deliverables," and your biography statement. These might take some time to draft and edit before submitting.

Cost: There should be no cost to you for speaking on this topic at a formal conference, panel event, etc. However, there will likely be a subsidized conference fee once your speaking proposal is accepted by the event planners. This is the reduced cost for speakers to enjoy the other activities comprising the event. For a speaker, the event registration cost can range from $100 to $400. Also, depending on your location and that of the event, you may have travel costs.

Tool 3: Grant Budgets Can Educate

What: Educate and advocate to funders so that they have the opportunity to do the right thing here. Present to the funders that your organization, program, and/or project must have one or more team wellness line items in the budget. Such line items equate to mission impact and, hopefully, mirrors your organization's outward and inward facing values. This tool is for those with grant writing responsibilities and in many organizations these responsibilities can be held by a program manager, executive director, or a Board chair. If this is not part of your set of tasks, then consider sharing this tool with colleagues who do have grant writing ahead of them.

Why this tool is important: The cost of staff time matters in terms of the organizational tools discussed earlier in this book. Yes, it is the duty of organizational leaders to implement those tools and to openly advocate for transforming the nonprofit sector culture and norms alive and living in your organization like an unwelcomed guest. Philanthropic entities do not understand nor fully hold space in their minds and hearts about the state of nonprofit community-based social services teams and ways that societal oppressions operate widely in organizations unless mitigating is invested in. That is, racism and classism don't just not happen because organizations don't want such oppressions to occur in their team. Of course the most historically oppressed team members, women, BIPOC persons, and the lowest paid, are going to be oppressed through the work structures and practices inside nonprofit organizations. Of course! But philanthropic entities are rarely on the up and up about these things (Villanueva, 2021).

How: In the required budget table, as grant writers and those with grant writing responsibilities know, include a line item for the staff time and resources required for implementation of the tools from the chapter on organizational tools and other related tools that you identify. There is often a word limit in grant applications. Where you are required, provide a few sentences that explains the line items, including any short data statement that is relevant. Be sure to describe the link between things like *capacity building* and the data on unmitigated chronic stress and vicarious trauma. Use whatever words that the funder is familiar with and/or expects to see such as *innovation, capacity building, impact assessment, quality assurance,* and maybe even *anti-racism, equitable treatment,* and *staff retention.* Budget line items typically reflect the following language:

- **Personnel and Benefits.** This is where you could include two things from the chapter on organization level tools. First, include Tool 9 which is focused on reassessing health and operational insurance plans to increase wellness resource bundles available to the team that can help to mitigate chronic stress and vicarious trauma. Second, Tool 1 is focused on unionizing your organization which can fold into this area of a budget based on your organization's discussion with the Nonprofit Professional Employees Union.
- **Consulting and Professional Costs.** This is where your organization could include three things. First, include a BIPOC consultant cost if your team believes that it is best to have a third-party facilitator support the completion of Approach 1 that functions as an opportunity to prime your organization before implementing the organization level tools. Second, include a BIPOC coach, reflecting Tool 2 in the chapter on organization level tools. Third, include a strategic planning specialist for Tool 11 discussed in the same chapter.
- **Materials and Supplies.** This is where you could include Tool 7 from the chapter on organizational tools for developing a staff retreat that involves solution-building around unmitigated chronic stress and vicarious trauma. Also, Tool 9 can be included in this type of budget area in terms of compensation alternatives informed by research studies on this topic and ensuring safety at your work site.
- **Computers and Technological Equipment.** This is where you could include Tool 3 from the chapter on organization level tools

to ensure that your organization has the needed payroll software for developing a transparent pay practice.

- **Printing and Publications.** This is where your organization can request funds that are generally supportive of the implementation of the tools indicated above.

The worst result for your implementation of this tool is that you educate the funder about the existence of the problem. The best result is that your organization receives fund to mitigate blowback from explosure to chronic stress and vicarious trauma.

Cost: The inclusion of the budget content focused on taking steps to mitigate the negative impact of chronic stress and vicarious trauma among your team will cost whatever your organization plans to spend on grant writing. If you are the grant writer, then the implementation of this tool is covered by your typical writing process. If your organization hires a grant writer or grant writing agency, be sure that you have a brainstorming session with the grant writer to ensure that this person appropriately implements this tool.

---

3 Sector Level Tools
Which tools will I, with allies, experiment with?

- ☐ Tool 1: *Write Intentional Letters*
- ☐ Tool 2: *Speak Widely*
- ☐ Tool 3: *Grant Budgets Can Educate*

What rhythm will I, with allies, use for implementing the tool(s)?

- ☐ **Place a calendar reminder to engage the tool(s) every month.**
- ☐ **Develop a group that implements the tool(s) together seasonally.**
- ☐ **Pass on these tools to colleagues and friends in the nonprofit sector.**

Reflections

Closing

Earlier in this book, we heard the voices of many nonprofit community-based social services professionals with direct-service roles. Qualitative survey feedback was especially insightful in terms of their existing individual approaches to coping with unmitigated chronic stress and vicarious trauma. Some shared approaches include, "Exercise, Netflix binges, Hulu shows, shopping, playing with my dogs, listening to music," and also "Therapy, decompress with friends, mindless phone games on the commute home, stay home from protests or other draining activism, loudly tell everyone I know that non-profits are just a feel-good tax shelter for the rich and will never achieve true systemic change." Their ideas about organizational actions to mitigate chronic stress and vicarious trauma are also important. We even got to see that for those with both supervisory and direct-service roles, they experienced higher rates of unmitigated chronic stress and vicarious trauma. This descriptive survey data, coupled with other research, illustrate the sector-wide reality of unmitigated chronic stress and vicarious trauma.

The 17 individual level tools presented in an earlier chapter can assist these professionals with research-backed and indigenous-based options while the racist and classist nonprofit foundation that drives unmitigated chronic stress and vicarious trauma is addressed at the organizational and sector levels. These individual tools are not replacements for shifting the sector. Our private activities and rituals do not rid racism and classism from being powerful influences; our private activities and rituals are for engaging some degree of wellbeing in a sea of suffering. The sector level tools described in this chapter are geared to educate the structural gatekeepers, current and future, who have large scopes of influence on topics like unmitigated chronic stress and vicarious trauma. These tools, as well as some of the 11 organizational level tools in the previous chapter, can be implemented on your own time or collectively with friends, colleagues, teams, and family.

While it is likely to take generations to end racism and classism in the U.S. (Menakem, 2017), making anti-racist headway in the nonprofit sector is our task today. It is not surprising to have the nonprofit sector inundated with racist and classist internal practices; the sector was founded through racist and classist agendas several hundred years old. White supremacy will not go away on its own; white supremacy's priority with inventing ideas and structural policies that propose that there are inferior heritage groups and class levels must be openly and consistently engaged with information and tools like this book offers. Mitigating chronic stress and vicarious trauma in nonprofit community-based organizations requires disassembling its norms that attempt to camouflage racism and classism as supposedly simply doing good for oppressed groups.

References

Abegun, D., and Stanciole, A. (2006). *An Estimation of the Economic Impact of Chronic Noncommunicable Diseases in Selected Countries*. Geneva: World Health Organization.

Alam, Shawkat. (2013). *Routledge Handbook of International Environmental Law*. New York: Routledge.

Albright, D.L., Fletcher, K.L., Pelts, M.D., & Taliaferro, L. (2017). Use of college mental health services among student veterans. *Best Practices in Mental Health, 13*(1), 66–80.

Allen, M., Wilhelm, A., Ortega, L.E., Pergament, S., Bates, N., & Cunningham, B. (2021). Applying a race (ism)-conscious adaptation of the CFIR Framework to understand implementation of a school-based equity-oriented intervention. *Ethnicity & Disease, 31*(Suppl), 375–388.

Aparicio, E., Michalopoulos, L.M., & Unick, G.J. (2013). An examination of the psychometric properties of the Vicarious Trauma Scale in a sample of licensed social workers. *Health & Social Work, 38*(4), 199–206.

Baines D., Hadley K., Slade B., et al. (2002). *Improving Work Organization to Reduce Injury and Illness: Social Services, Stress, Violence and Workload*. Hamilton, Ontario, Canada: Institute for Work in a Global Society.

Bartczak, L. (2015). Building collaboration from the inside out. Washington, D.C.: Grantmakers for Effective Organizations.

Baum, Andrew, & Posluszny, Donna M. (1999). Health Psychology: Mapping Biobehavioral Contributions to Health and Illness. *Annual Review of Psychology, 50*(1), 137–163.

Beemsterboer, W., Stewart, R., Groothoff, J., & Nijhuis, F. (2009). A literature review on sick leave determinants (1984–2004). *International Journal of Occupational Medicine and Environmental Health, 22*(2), 169–179.

Benoit, C., McCarthy, B., & Jansson, M. (2015). Occupational stigma and mental health: Discrimination and depression among front-line service workers. *Canadian Public Policy, 41*(Supplement 2), S61-S69.

Bittman, B.B., Berk, L.S., Felten, D.L., & Westengard, J. (2001). Composite effects of group drumming music therapy on modulation of neuroendocrine-immune parameters in normal subjects. *Alternative Therapies in Health and Medicine, 7*(1), 38.

Bonilla-Silva, Eduardo. *Racism without Racists: Color-blind Racism and the Persistence of Racial Inequality in the United States*. 2nd ed. Lanham: Rowman & Littlefield, 2006. Print.

Branson, D.C. (2019). Vicarious Trauma, Themes in Research, and Terminology: A Review of Literature. *Traumatology (Tallahassee, Fla.), 25*(1), 2–10.

Bremner, J.D., Mishra, S., Campanella, C., Shah, M., Kasher, N., Evans, S., ... & Vaccarino, V. (2017). A pilot study of the effects of mindfulness-based stress reduction on post-traumatic stress disorder symptoms and brain response to traumatic reminders of combat in Operation Enduring Freedom/Operation Iraqi Freedom combat veterans with post-traumatic stress disorder. *Frontiers in Psychiatry, 8*, 157.

Bubonya, M., Cobb-Clark, D.A., & Wooden, M. (2017). Mental health and

References

productivity at work: Does what you do matter? *Labour Economics, 46*, 150–165.

Burrell, Q.L. (1985). The 80/20 rule: Library lore or statistical law? *Journal of Documentation.*

Castilla, E.J. (2015). Accounting for the gap: A firm study manipulating organizational accountability and transparency in pay decisions. *Organization Science, 26*(2), 311–333.

CBS News Productions, production company. (2013). *Movies: Short Term 12.* Columbia Broadcasting System.

Chaco, E. (2021). Mentorship, Leadership and Being an Indigenous Woman. *Journal of Legal Education, 69*(3), 4.

Chan, C.D., Harrichand, J.J., Anandavalli, S., Vaishnav, S., Chang, C.Y., Hyun, J.H., & Band, M.P. (2021). Mapping solidarity, liberation, and activism: A critical autoethnography of Asian American leaders in counseling. *Journal of Mental Health Counseling, 43*(3), 246–265.

Choi, B., Ahn, S., & Lee, S. (2017). Construction Workers' Group Norms and Personal Standards Regarding Safety Behavior: Social Identity Theory Perspective. *Journal of Management in Engineering, 33*(4), 1–11.

Cobas, José A., Jorge. Duany, and Joe R. Feagin. (2009). *How the United States Racializes Latinos: White Hegemony and Its Consequences.* Boulder: Paradigm.

Coddington, Kate. (2017). Contagious Trauma: Reframing the Spatial Mobility of Trauma within Advocacy Work. *Emotion, Space and Society, 24.C*: 66–73. Web.

Coe, I.R., Wiley, R., & Bekker, L.G. (2019). Organizational best practices towards gender equality in science and medicine. *The Lancet, 393*(10171), 587–593.

Creech, S.K., & Misca, G. (2017). Parenting with PTSD: A review of research on the influence of PTSD on parent-child functioning in military and veteran families. *Frontiers in Psychology, 8*, 1101.

Crile, G. (2003). *Charlie Wilson's War: The Extraordinary Story of How the Wildest Man in Congress and a Rogue CIA Agent Changed the History of Our Times.* Grove Press.

Crutchfield, L.R., & Grant, H.M. (2012). *Forces for Good: The Six Practices of High-Impact Nonprofits.* John Wiley & Sons.

Cuddy, A.J.C., Fiske, S.T., & Glick, P. (2004). When professionals become mothers, warmth doesn't cut the ice. *Journal of Social Issues, 60*(4), 701–718.

Curry, S.R., Baiocchi, A., Tully, B.A., Garst, N., Bielz, S., Kugley, S., & Morton, M.H. (2020). Improving program implementation and client engagement in interventions addressing youth homelessness: A meta-synthesis. *Children and Youth Services Review, 105691.*

Davis, L.L., Whetsell, C., Hamner, M.B., Carmody, J., Rothbaum, B.O., Allen, R.S., ... & Bremner, J.D. (2019). A multisite randomized controlled trial of mindfulness-based stress reduction in the treatment of posttraumatic stress disorder. *Psychiatric Research and Clinical Practice, 1*(2), 39–48.

Demerouti, E. (2015). Strategies used by individuals to prevent burnout. *European Journal of Clinical Investigation, 45*(10), 1106–1112.

DiAngelo, R. (2021). *Nice Racism: How Progressive White People Perpetuate Racial Harm.* Beacon Press.

DiAngelo, R. (2018). *White Fragility: Why It's So Hard for White People to Talk About Racism.* Beacon Press.

Duarte, J., & Pinto-Gouveia, J. (2017). Empathy and feelings of guilt experienced by nurses: A cross-sectional study of their role in burnout and compassion fatigue symptoms. *Applied Nursing Research, 35*, 42–47.

Dunbar-Ortiz, R. (2014). *An Indigenous Peoples' History of the United States.* Beacon Press.

Eagly, A.H., & Karau, S.J. (2002). Role congruity theory of prejudice toward female leaders. *Psychological Review, 109*, 573–598.

Eller, E., and Frey, D. (2018) The Group Effect: Social Influences on Risk Identification, Analysis, and Decision Making. In: Raue M., Lermer E., Streicher B. (eds) *Psychological Perspectives on Risk and Risk Analysis.* Springer, Cham

Elrod, J.K., & Fortenberry, J.L. (2017). The hub-and-spoke organization design: an

References

avenue for serving patients well. *BMC Health Services Research, 17*(1), 25–33.

Espelage, D.L., Merrin, G.J., & Hatchel, T. (2018). Peer victimization and dating violence among LGBTQ youth: The impact of school violence and crime on mental health outcomes. *Youth Violence and Juvenile Justice, 16*(2), 156–173.

Formanowicz, M., Bedynska, S., Cislak, A., Braun, F., & Sczesny, S. (2013). Side effects of gender-fair language: How feminine job titles influence the evaluation of female applicants. *European Journal of Social Psychology, 43*(1), 62–71.

Fortney, J.C., Curran, G.M., Hunt, J.B., Cheney, A.M., Lu, L., Valenstein, M., & Eisenberg, D. (2016). Prevalence of probable mental disorders and help-seeking behaviors among veteran and non-veteran community college students. *General Hospital Psychiatry, 38*, 99–104.

Giving USA (2018). *The Annual Report on Philanthropy for the Year 2017.* Chicago: Giving USA Foundation.

Gorski, P.C. (2015). Relieving Burnout and the "Martyr Syndrome" Among Social Justice Education Activists: The Implications and Effects of Mindfulness. *The Urban Review, 47*(4), 696–716.

Gorski, Paul C., & Erakat, Noura. (2019). Racism, whiteness, and burnout in anti-racism movements: How white racial justice activists elevate burnout in racial justice activists of color in the United States. *Ethnicities, 19*(5), 784–808.

Gottlieb, Hildy. (2009). 6 Reasons to Use the Term "Community Benefit Organization." Creating the Future. https://creatingthefuture.org/6-reasons-to-use-the-term-community-benefit-organization/

Graham, J. (2012). Cognitive behavioural therapy for occupational trauma: A systematic literature review exploring the effects of occupational trauma and the existing CBT support pathways and interventions for staff working within mental healthcare including allied professions. *The Cognitive Behaviour Therapist, 5*(1), 24–45.

Gramsci, A. (2010). Intellectuals and hegemony. In C. Lemert (Ed.), *Social theory: The Multicultural and Classic Readings* (pp. 263–265). Boulder, Colorado: Westview.

Greene, G.J., Fisher, K.A., Kuper, L., Andrews, R., & Mustanski, B. (2015). "Is this normal? Is this not normal? There is no set example": Sexual health intervention preferences of LGBT youth in romantic relationships. *Sexuality Research and Social Policy, 12*(1), 1–14.

Grise-Owens, Erlene, Miller, Justin "Jay," Escobar-Ratliff, Laura, & George, Nicole. (2017). Teaching Note—Teaching Self-Care and Wellness as a Professional Practice Skill: A Curricular Case Example. *Journal of Social Work Education, 54*(1), 180–186.

Gross, N., & Mann, M. (2017). Is there a "Ferguson effect?" Google searches, concern about police violence, and crime in U.S. cities, 2014–2016. *Socius, 3,*

Guastello, S., & Frampton, S.B. (2014). Patient-centered care retreats as a method for enhancing and sustaining compassion in action in healthcare settings. *Journal of Compassionate Health Care, 1*(1), 1–6.

Hacking, I. (1999). *The Social Construction of What?* Cambridge, Mass: Harvard University Press.

Hagerty, Michael. (2018). Mariachi Opera Tells of an Immigrant Family Divided by the Border. *Houston Public Media.* https://www.houstonpublicmedia.org/articles/arts-culture/2018/05/16/285617/mariachi-opera-tells-of-an-immigrant-family-divided-by-the-border/

Hallett, K., Fassinger, R., Miles-Cohen, S., Burrwell, T., Ward, E., & Wisdom, J. (2018). *The Changing Gender Composition of Professions: Lessons for Psychology.* (pp. 403–421). American Psychological Association.

Harvey, Sean P., and Sarah Rivett. "Colonial-Indigenous Language Encounters in North America and the Intellectual History of the Atlantic World." *Early American Studies: An Interdisciplinary Journal* 15.3 (2017): 442–73. Web.

Haslam, S.A. (2014). Making good theory practical: Five lessons for an Applied

References

Social Identity Approach to challenges of organizational, health, and clinical psychology. *British Journal of Social Psychology*, 53(1), 1–20. https://doi.org/10.1111/bjso.12061

Harzer, C., & Ruch, W. (2015). The relationships of character strengths with coping, work-related stress, and job satisfaction. *Frontiers in Psychology*, 6, 165.

Haslam, C., & Cook, M. (2002). Striking a chord with amnesic patients: Evidence that song facilitates memory. *Neurocase*, 8(6), 453–465.

Hernandez-Wolfe, Pilar, Killian, Kyle, Engstrom, David, & Gangsei, David. (2014). Vicarious Resilience, Vicarious Trauma, and Awareness of Equity in Trauma Work. *The Journal of Humanistic Psychology*, 55(2), 153–172.

Hewlin, Patricia Faison, Sung Soo Kim, and Young Ho Song. "Creating Facades of Conformity in the Face of Job Insecurity: A Study of Consequences and Conditions." *Journal of Occupational and Organizational Psychology* 89.3 (2016): 539–67. Web.

Hoemberg, V. (2005). Evidence based medicine in neurological rehabilitation—A critical review. *Re-Engineering of the Damaged Brain and Spinal Cord*, 3–14.

Holness, D., Somerville, S., Kosny, A., Gadeski, J., Mastandrea, J., & Sinclair, G. (2004). Workplace health and safety concerns in service organizations in the inner city. *Journal of Urban Health*, 81(3): 489–97.

Hotchkiss, J.T. (2018). Mindful self-care and secondary traumatic stress mediate a relationship between compassion satisfaction and burnout risk among hospice care professionals. *American Journal of Hospice and Palliative Medicine*®, 35(8), 1099–1108.

Hoyt, C.L. (2012). Gender bias in employment contexts: A closer examination of the role incongruity principle. *Journal of Experimental Social Psychology*, 48 (1), 86–96.

Hunsaker, S., Chen, H.C., Maughan, D., & Heaston, S. (2015). Factors that influence the development of compassion fatigue, burnout, and compassion satisfaction in emergency department nurses. *Journal of Nursing Scholarship*, 47(2), 186–194.

Huyghebaert, T., Gillet, N., Fernet, C., Lahiani, F.J., & Fouquereau, E. (2018). Leveraging psychosocial safety climate to prevent ill-being: The mediating role of psychological need thwarting. *Journal of Vocational Behavior*, 107, 111–125.

Impellizzeri, F., Leonardi, S., Latella, D., Maggio, M.G., Cuzzola, M.F., Russo, M., ... & Calabrò, R.S. (2020). An integrative cognitive rehabilitation using neurologic music therapy in multiple sclerosis: A pilot study. *Medicine*, 99 (4).

Infobase, film distributor, & PBS. (2019). *Trafficked in America*. PBS.

Jonassen, D.H. & Kim, B. (2010). Arguing to learn and learning to argue: Design justifications and guidelines. *Educational Technology Research and Development*, 58(4), 439–457.

Johns Hopkins, C.S.S.E. (2020). Coronavirus COVID-19 Global Cases by the Center for Systems Science and Engineering (CSSE) at Johns Hopkins University (JHU). *Dipetik* April, 19, 2020. https://coronavirus.jhu.edu/map.html

Kanter, B., & Sherman, A. (2017). *The Happy, Healthy Nonprofit: Strategies for Impact Without Burnout*. Hoboken, New Jersey: Wiley.

Kearney, E.M. (2013). Studying Successful Teachers. In *On Becoming a Teacher* (pp. 91–95). Brill Sense.

Kelleher, F., Severin, F.O., Unesco, & Commonwealth Secretariat. (2011). *Women and the Teaching Profession: Exploring the Feminization Debate*. London: Commonwealth Secretariat.

Keeney, B. (2004). *Bushman Shaman: Awakening the Spirit Through Ecstatic Dance*. Simon & Schuster.

Keeney, B. (2007). *Shaking Medicine: The Healing Power of Ecstatic Movement*. Simon & Schuster.

Kim, S.C., & Sekol, M.A. (2014). Job satisfaction, burnout, and stress among pediatric nurses in various specialty units at an acute care hospital.

Kisner, J. (2017). The politics of conspicuous displays of self-care. *The New Yorker*, 14.

References

Knuckey, Sarah, Margaret Satterthwaite, and Adam Brown. "Trauma, Depression, and Burnout in the Human Rights Field: Identifying Barriers and Pathways to Resilient Advocacy." *Columbia Human Rights Law Review* 49.3 (2018): 267–323. Web.

Kristensen, T.S., Borritz, M., Villadsen, E., & Christensen, K.B. (2005). The Copenhagen Burnout Inventory: A new tool for the assessment of burnout. *Work & Stress, 19*(3), 192–207.

Lampert, B., & Glaser, J. (2018). Detached concern in client interaction and burnout. *International Journal of Stress Management, 25*(2), 129.

Lawlor, Jennifer A., Bronwyn A. Hunter, Leonard A. Jason, and Howard B. Rosing. (2014) Natural Mentoring in Oxford House Recovery Homes: A Preliminary Analysis. *Journal of Groups in Addiction & Recovery,* 9.2: 126–42.

Lazaridis, K., Jovanović, J., Jovanović, J., Šarac, I., & Jovanović, S. (2017). The impact of occupational stress factors on temporary work disability related to arterial hypertension and its complications. *International Journal of Occupational Safety and Ergonomics, 23*(2), 259–266.

Lehavot, K., Katon, J.G., Chen, J.A., Fortney, J.C., & Simpson, T.L. (2018). Post-traumatic stress disorder by gender and veteran status. *American Journal of Preventive Medicine, 54*(1), e1-e9.

Lemmen, N. H., Keizer, K., Bouman, T., & Steg, L. (2020). Convince yourself to do the right thing: The effects of provided versus self-generated arguments on rule compliance and perceived importance of socially desirable behavior. *Frontiers in Psychology, 11,* 3608.

Lester M. Salamon, & S. Wojciech Sokolowski. (2015). The Resilient Sector Revisited (2nd ed.). Brookings Institution Press.

Liana Loewus (2017). The Nation's Teaching Force Is Still Mostly White and Female, Education Week. https://www.edweek.org/ew/articles/2017/08/15/the-nations-teaching-force-is-still-mostly.html Retrieved 11/31/2019

Lindsay, S., & Edwards, A. (2013). A systematic review of disability awareness interventions for children and youth. *Disability and Rehabilitation, 35*(8), 623–646.

Lipsky, L. van D. (2018). *The Age of Overwhelm: Strategies for the Long Haul.* Berrett-Koehler Publishers.

Lorde, A. (1979). *Sister Outsider: Essays and Speeches.* Sister Vision Press. Toronto, Canada.

Lu, L., Lu, A.C.C., Gursoy, D., & Neale, N.R. (2016). Work engagement, job satisfaction, and turnover intentions: A comparison between supervisors and line-level employees. *International Journal of Contemporary Hospitality Management.*

Ludick, Marné, & Figley, Charles R. (2017). Toward a Mechanism for Secondary Trauma Induction and Reduction: Reimagining a Theory of Secondary Traumatic Stress. *Traumatology (Tallahassee, Fla.), 23*(1), 112–123.

Mananzala, R., & Spade, D. (2008). The nonprofit industrial complex and trans resistance. *Sexuality Research & Social Policy, 5*(1), 53.

Marmot, M. (2015). *The Health Gap: The Challenge of an Unequal World.* London, UK: Bloomsbury.

Marzec, M. L., Scibelli, A., & Edington, D. (2015). Impact of changes in medical condition burden index and stress on absenteeism among employees of a U.S. utility company. *International Journal of Workplace Health Management.*

McCarthy, Singer, Sugar, Golin, Rocklin, Faust, Ruffalo, Keaton, McAdams, Schreiber, Slattery, James, Tucci, Crudup, Guilfoyle, Sheridan, Cariou, Huff, Creighton, ... McArdle. (2015). *Spotlight.* Universal Studios Home Entertainment.

McCarthy, M., Bates, C., Triantafyllopoulou, P., Hunt, S., & Milne Skillman, K. (2019). "Put bluntly, they are targeted by the worst creeps society has to offer": Police and professionals' views and actions relating to domestic violence and women with intellectual disabilities. *Journal of Applied Research in Intellectual Disabilities, 32*(1), 71–81.

McDaniel, Sara, and Anna-Margaret Yarbrough. (2016). A Literature Review of

References

Afterschool Mentoring Programs for Children at Risk. *Journal of At-Risk Issues,* 19.1: 1–9.

Meiksins, Rob. (2019). Nonprofit Workers Find Fulfillment through "Us," not "Me." Nonprofit Quarterly. https://nonprofitquarterly.org/nonprofit-workers-find-fulfillment-through-us-not-me/

Menakem, Resmaa. (2017). *My Grandmother's Hands: Racialized Trauma and the Pathway to Mending Our Hearts and Bodies.* Penguin UK.

Mitchell, K. (2018). Identifying White Mediocrity and Know-Your-Place Aggression: A Form of Self-Care. *African American Review, 51*(4), 253–262.

Mont, S. (2017). The future of nonprofit leadership: Worker self-directed organizations. *Non Profit News / Nonprofit Quarterly.*

Morgan, Amy J, Ross, Anna, & Reavley, Nicola J. (2018). Systematic review and meta-analysis of Mental Health First Aid training: Effects on knowledge, stigma, and helping behaviour. *PloS One, 13*(5), e0197102–e0197102.

Morgan, K. (2017). Parole Process and Practice. In *Routledge Handbook of Corrections in the United States* (pp. 165–178). Routledge.

Morrissette, Ann-Sophie (2016, Oct 31). Five Myths that Perpetuate Burnout Across Nonprofits. *Stanford Social Innovation Review.* https://ssir.org/articles/entry/five_myths_that_perpetuate_burnout_across_nonprofits#

Naurin, E., and Ohberg, P. (2013). Call Me Maybe? Politicians' Views of Citizen-Initiated Contacts with Elected Representatives. A Survey and Experiment with Swedish Politicians. *Stepping Stones, 77.*

Newhouse, Chelsea. (2018). Nonprofits: America's Third Largest Workforce. Johns Hopkins Center for Civil Society Studies. https://ccss.jhu.edu/2015-np-employment-report/

Nodoushani, O., Carol Stewart, & Emily J Gallagher. (2019). Another Outlook towards the U.S. Nonprofit Sector Segments. *Competition Forum, 17*(1), 145–151.

Okun, Tema. (n.d.). White Supremacy Culture. www.DismantlingRacism.org.

Page, M. (2017). Forgotten youth: Homeless LGBT youth of color and the Runaway and Homeless Youth Act. *Northwestern Journal of Law & Social Policy, 12*(2), 17.

Page, N.C., & Nilsson, V.O. (2017). Active commuting: workplace health promotion for improved employee well-being and organizational behavior. *Frontiers in Psychology, 7.*

Perez-Truglia, R. (2020). The effects of income transparency on well-being: Evidence from a natural experiment. *American Economic Review, 110*(4), 1019–54.

Phillips, R., Benoit, C., Hallgrimsdottir, H., & Vallance, K. (2012). Courtesy stigma: A hidden health concern among front-line service providers to sex workers. *Sociology of Health & Illness, 34*(5), 681–696.

Putney, C. (2009). *Muscular Christianity: Manhood and Sports in Protestant America, 1880–1920.* Harvard University Press.

Quach, J., & Lee, J.A. (2017). Do music therapies reduce depressive symptoms and improve QOL in older adults with chronic disease? *Nursing2020, 47*(6), 58–63.

Raja, U., Javed, Y., & Abbas, M. (2018). A time lagged study of burnout as a mediator in the relationship between workplace bullying and work-family conflict. *International Journal of Stress Management, 25*(4), 377.

Rodrigues, C.C.F. M., Santos, V.E.P., & Sousa, P. (2017). Patient safety and nursing: interface with stress and Burnout Syndrome. *Revista Brasileira de Enfermagem, 70*(5), 1083–1088.

Rogers, H. (2014). Kindness and reciprocity: liberated prisoners and Christian charity in early nineteenth-century England. *Journal of Social History, 47*(3), 721–745.

Rojiani, R., Junn, A., Wood, M., Gordon, K.L., & Sells, D. (2021). Group drumming for incarcerated men may improve community reintegration: a mixed methods pilot study. *Journal of Experimental Criminology,* 1–22.

References

Rzeszutek, Marcin, Partyka, Małgorzata, & Gołąb, Andrzej. (2015). Temperament Traits, Social Support, and Secondary Traumatic Stress Disorder Symptoms in a Sample of Trauma Therapists. *Professional Psychology, Research and Practice, 46*(4), 213–220.

Saad, Layla (2020). Me and White Supremacy: Combat Racism, Change the World, and Become a Good Ancestor. Sourcebooks: Naperville, Illinois.

Schroder, H.S., Yalch, M.M., Dawood, S., Callahan, C.P., Donnellan, M.B., & Moser, J.S. (2017). Growth mindset of anxiety buffers the link between stressful life events and psychological distress and coping strategies. *Personality and Individual Differences, 110*, 23–26.

Seti, C. (2008). Causes and Treatment of Burnout in Residential Child Care Workers: A Review of the Research. Residential Treatment for Children & Youth, 24(3), 197–229.

Shakespeare-Finch, J., & Daley, E. (2017). Workplace belongingness, distress, and resilience in emergency service workers. *Psychological Trauma: Theory, Research, Practice, and Policy, 9*(1), 32–35.

Shakespeare-Finch, Jane, Amanda Rees, & Deanne Armstrong. (2015). Social Support, Self-efficacy, Trauma and Well-Being in Emergency Medical Dispatchers. *Social Indicators Research, 123*(2), 549–565.

Shanafelt, T.D., Gorringe, G., Menaker, R., Storz, K.A., Reeves, D., Buskirk, S.J., ... & Swensen, S.J. (2015, April). Impact of organizational leadership on physician burnout and satisfaction. In *Mayo Clinic Proceedings*, 90(4), 432–440. Elsevier.

Shear, S.B., Knowles, R.T., Soden, G.J., & Castro, A.J. (2015). Manifesting destiny: Re/presentations of indigenous peoples in K–12 US history standards. *Theory & Research in Social Education, 43*(1), 68–101.

Shelden, R. & Vélez Young, M. (2021). Our punitive society: Race, class, gender, and punishment in America. Waveland Press: Long Grove: Illinois.

Sewell, A.A. (2017, December). The illness associations of police violence: Differential relationships by ethnoracial composition. In *Sociological Forum, 32*, 975–997.

Skovholt, T.M., & Trotter-Mathison, M. (2011). The resilient practitioner: Burnout prevention and self-care strategies for counselors, therapists, teachers, and health professionals. New York: Routledge.

Smith, C., Viljoen, J.T., & McGeachie, L. (2014). African drumming: a holistic approach to reducing stress and improving health? *Journal of Cardiovascular Medicine, 15*(6), 441–446.

Sollie, H., Kop, N., & Euwema, M.C. (2017). Mental resilience of crime scene investigators: How police officers perceive and cope with the impact of demanding work situations. *Criminal Justice and Behavior, 44*(12), 1580–1603.

Spigt, M., Weerkamp, N., Troost, J., van Schayck, C.P., & Knottnerus, J.A. (2012). A randomized trial on the effects of regular water intake in patients with recurrent headaches. *Family Practice, 29*(4), 370–375.

Struthers, R. and Eschiti, V.S. (2005). Being healed by an indigenous traditional healer: sacred healing stories of Native Americans. Part II. *Complementary Therapies in Clinical Practice, 11*(2), 78–86.

Sumner, Steven A, Mercy, James A, Dahlberg, Linda L, Hillis, Susan D, Klevens, Joanne, & Houry, Debra. (2015). Violence in the United States: Status, Challenges, and Opportunities. *JAMA: The Journal of the American Medical Association, 314*(5), 478–488.

Taylor, B. G., & Mumford, E.A. (2016). A national descriptive portrait of adolescent relationship abuse: Results from the National Survey on Teen Relationships and Intimate Violence. *Journal of Interpersonal Violence, 31*(6), 963–988.

Thaut, M., Gardiner, J., Holmberg, D., Horwitz, J., Kent, L., Andrews, G., ... & Mcintosh, G. (2009). Neurologic music therapy improves executive function

References

and emotional adjustment in traumatic brain injury rehabilitation. *Annals of the New York Academy of Sciences, 1169*(1), 406–416.

Thornton, C. (2007). The revolution will not be funded: Beyond the nonprofit industrial complex. *NACLA Report on the Americas, 40*(4), 49.

Timm, J. (2016). The plight of the overworked nonprofit employee. *The Atlantic.*

Tsunogaya, N., Sugahara, S., & Chand, P. (2017). The impact of social influence pressures, commitment, and personality on judgments by auditors: evidence from Japan. *Journal of International Accounting Research, 16*(3), 17–34.

Universal Pictures. *(2007). Charlie Wilson's War.* Universal City, California: Universal Studios Home Entertainment.

Villanueva, E. (2021). *Decolonizing Wealth: Indigenous Wisdom to Heal Divides and Restore Balance.* Berrett-Koehler Publishers.

Ware, Nat. (2013). Free Charities from The Idea of Charity. Tedx Talks. https://www.youtube.com/watch?v=Zpzvnbsma2U

Wheeler, Juanita. (2015). Busting the Charity Overhead Myth. Tedx Talks. https://www.youtube.com/watch?v=0diX8FHOKZE

Wilkins, E. (2016). Dispelling the myths around chronic fatigue. *Occupational Health & Wellbeing, 68*(6), 19.

Word, J., Norton, L., Davis, S., & Nguyen, A. (2011). Engaging the nonprofit workforce: Mission, management and emotion. *Opportunity Knocks.*

Index

Index

transparent pay 135

unionizing 91, 133

veterans 67–68
vicarious trauma 11, 49, 65, 124; health
  consequences of 18, 60–61, 122

walking meetings 100–101
water 101–102
white supremacy 9

yoga 113, 114